BIRTHMARKED FOR GLORY AND HONOR:

BREAKING THE CURSE OF ICHABOD

By APOSTLE KELLY MCCANN

Manuscript Editor: K.M., Keturah Rosato, J.M
Cover Designer: Dawn Fisher
Foreword - Apostle Walt Healy

All scripture quotations are taken from many translations:
New King James Version (NKJV)
The Message Bible (TMB)
New International Version (NIV)
New American Standard Bible (NASB)
The Amplified Bible (AMP)
King James Version (KJV)

BOOK DEDICATION PAGE

I would like to dedicate this book and say 'THANK YOU" to all those deliverance, inner healing, and outer healing ministers, locally, regionally, in and out of the state, and around the globe, that get up every day and say: "Somebody captive comes out of their stuck place today!", or "Somebody bound to addiction comes into liberty and wholeness today"!, or "Somebody in chronic pain will be divinely healed and have the life that Jesus died to give them."! This is to recognize all of those who are writing, speaking, praying, prophesying, preaching, teaching, and standing fearlessly in the trenches with the wounded, the broken, the outcasts, the hurting, and the captive. To all of those in the army of God, that selflessly give days, weeks, and years of their lives, that they could be spending one thousand other ways, but choose to pour their time, effort, energy, focus, and anointing on, laying down their lives, so that others can come up in theirs; I say, Thank You for giving to the Lord. So many lives are changed because of your fearless obedience. Stay strong in the Lord and the power of his might, my comrades!!!

I would also like to thank my amazing husband, James, for all of his support and help with everything in my life. I could not do what I do without you, Babe. I would also like to thank my children, Matthew, Gabriel, Victoria, Jessica, and grandbabies, Joey and Francesca for making my life beautiful. I love you all so much.

Thank you Apostle Walt Healy, for being such an inspiration. You love God and the Word of God and you make everyone around you more hungry to know God and know His Word. Living by faith is a lifestyle for you and you live it out in and out of the podium. I am so thankful for a kingdom connection and for your mentoring in my life.

Thank you to Apostle Leo Fram, Apostle Edith Fram, and Apostle Michael Fram. You are my spiritual family, and I am so glad that God connected us for Kingdom purposes and to model a godly family that is truly there for you whenever you need them and to be a safe haven when things get difficult or when I need answers to real life questions.

TABLE OF CONTENTS

PREFACE

In the military, they use a couple of different packs for their assignments. One of these packs is called a rucksack – which is a backpack used for long missions with lots of equipment in it. Another type of pack is an assault pack – which is a backpack with a few things in it for a short-targeted mission. In an assault pack, there are less things, all used in a shorter period of time. This book is an assault pack against the world, the flesh and the devil. It will bring accelerated healing, deliverance, and growth. Although there are lots of artillery in this book, I believe that we are in a season where acceleration of God's timetable is happening in the earth. History is His Story—and we have to know our place, authority, and assignment in it for such a time as this. There is an old saying, "If you don't have an opinion, I'll give you one." If we don't know what God has created us for, we will allow the opinions of others to direct us instead of God himself.

God's opinion of you is that you were marked for glory and honor, before you were ever conceived and known and marked by your parents, siblings, friends, or other people who have influenced your view of who you are. How do I know that? I'm glad you asked. Ephesians 1:4 says, "For he chose us in him before the creation of the world to be holy and blameless in his sight. In love, he predestined us for adoption to sonship through Jesus Christ, in accordance with his pleasure and will—to the praise of his glorious grace, which he has freely given us in the One he loves. In him we have redemption through his blood, the forgiveness of sins, in accordance with the riches of God's grace that he lavished on us." So God chose you first!! You did not choose him, he chose you first! That is why you are here on the earth. He created you and crowned you with glory—meaning the inherited glory from our being created in Gods image. (1 Cor. 11:7). So what is God's glory? It is the Hebrew word, 'Kabad", which means weight or heaviness. The same word is then used to express importance, honor and majesty. So Biblical honor is defined as "Kabad" meaning the weightiness of God, the manifest Presence of God and the glory of God. We are all products of God's love and glory through the finished work of the cross. Now this is the truth about who you are and where you came from, but we are going to look at where the lie that says, "Ichabod" over you, which means, "the glory of God has departed from you" began, how we need to come out of agreement with this lie, and how to replace it with the truth of what God says about us, and then decree the truth over ourselves on a regular basis.

FOREWORD BY APOSTLE WALT HEALY

I applaud Kelly McCann's effort in her new book to shatter the lies that hold so many believers back from being "partakers of the divine nature" (2 Pt.1:4). Toxic beliefs implanted by the world and sometimes even a misinformed church have to be removed; only then will the word of God find entrance at the heart level where one believes and then releases with the mouth into salvation (the abundant life Christ has secured for us, spirit, soul and body) Rom.10:9,10.

In this book you will find practical application of God's truth set out in simple ways which can be easily followed. Too often, we hear the truth but don't know how to abide in it (live in it; dwell in it). Jesus explained in John 8:31-32 that abiding in His word actuates the ability to "know the truth, and the truth shall make you free". This word "know" is one of eight terms for "knowing" and signifies knowing experientially.

Kelly will help you find this freedom which is revealed as: You in Christ (seated in heavenly places); and Christ in you (here on earth), the hope of glory now and forever.

As you connect with who you are in Christ, seated above every throne, dominion, power, authority, and name, then Christ, the burden bearing, yoke destroying Anointed One, will be revealed in you. This is the great mystery hidden in past ages but now revealed in Christ. In Christ is your identity; Christ in you is your victory!

INTRODUCTION

"You Have Arrived"! Don't we all just love to hear those words from our GPS? That joyous exhale moment comes, and the blood rushes back in our faces, when, after we have driven a long distance, have gotten lost and stopped at countless gas stations for directions, many Dunkin' Donuts for more coffee to deal with the stress of getting lost, and have made at least three frustrating calls to those people we are going to see. After word cursing others on the road that have cut us off, we can finally, in front of our arrived destination, do self-deliverance over our spirit of road rage, and finally arrive at our destination so we can return to "the joy of our salvation."

A GPS for driving, which is defined as a Global Positioning System, is a worldwide radio-navigation system formed from a constellation of 24 satellites and their ground stations. We also have a spiritual GPS-or a God Positioning System that God has had for us, from before the foundations of the world. God has a position for us to build his Kingdom, and God has a position of who we are in His Kingdom. So you were created for a specific purpose. You are not here by accident. Ephesians 2:10 says, "For we are his workmanship, created in Christ Jesus for good works, which God prepared beforehand, that we should walk in them." (ESV)

You were created for a specific wonderful plan. "Jeremiah 1:4 & 5 says, "Before you were born, I knew you, before you were born, I set you apart; I appointed you as a prophet to the nations." (NIV) So God set you apart and knew the awesome plan he had for your life before your parents or anybody else met you or connected with you. The plan that God has for you is a good plan. Jeremiah 29:11, says, "I know the thoughts I have toward you—plans to give you a future and a hope—an expected end." (NIV) So here we plainly see that God has thoughts of peace towards you. Do you believe God likes you? Because this scripture right here tells you what God thinks about you. God is saying, "I'm not thinking evil towards you, I am thinking peace. So if you are getting thoughts that are evil towards you, they are clearly not coming from God.

God is not trying to kill you. There are so many thoughts that we have to delete that are not of God. God said in this verse in Jeremiah that your thoughts and your expected end are connected. I submit to you that you CANNOT END ANY BETTER THEN YOU THINK!!! Our thinking has to be on God's Positioning System—we have to think about us what he thinks about us. Can you say these words, "God likes me". "God has a good plan for me". "God is not thinking bad thoughts toward me today or any day." One of the goals of this book is to get a resurrected thought life. We are going to do a mental detox as we progress throughout this book.

You were created in God's image. Gen. 1:26, 2:7, says, "Let us make man in our own image." Everything in these texts of Genesis 1 and 2 tells us about the intimate actions of God in creating mankind compared to everything else in creation.

Because God is spirit, it is the spirit portion of our triune being that worships and communes with God, discerns good and evil, and possesses divine authority to pull heaven down in to earth. John 2:24, "God is spirit, and they that worship him must worship him in spirit and in truth." Throughout this book, there are times when I am going to have you close your eyes and call your spirit forward to connect with God's spirit and then release a blessing or a decree over your own spirit. Many times I will have you pray, "I bless my spirit to remember"...and then go into a blessing or a decree taken from the Word of God so that you can be strengthened in your spirit by the truth. Our spirit man should always be in the driver's seat driving the car of our lives. And our soul—our own mind, will and emotion, should always be in the passenger seat, strapped in, to see where our spirit, guided by the Holy Spirit, will bring us to. As long as our spirit man is in the driver's seat being guided by the Holy Spirit, then our soul realm will be renewed in the knowledge of the Lord and we will be on the right track in our thinking. The power of these blessings will also cause your heart to expect to be blessed, especially where the Ichabod curse has created an unhealthy, toxic pattern in your life.

Ephesians 2:6, says, And God raised us up with Christ and seated us with him in the heavenly realms in Christ Jesus." This is evidence of our God Positioning System. Because of our belief in Christ, our spirit man is seated in heavenly places in Christ and when we intentionally pray and call our spirit man to connect with the Holy Spirit and take us up in our thinking to the way that Christ thinks, then we can see, from the top-down, where the enemy has had a legal right to steal from us, and we can see things through God's perspective again. God's positioning system will never bring confusion—only clarity of mind and real answers and peace. Peace is the soil of revelation. If we have no peace of mind, we cannot receive revelation from God. 3 John 2 says: " I wish that you would be in good health, even as your soul prospers". As your soul is healed, your body will be healed.

God has crowned you with glory and honor. David expresses in Psalm 8 his wonder at God making man with such glory and honor. Psalm 8:4-6 says, "What is man that you are mindful of them? You have made them a little lower than the angels and crowned them with glory and honor". You made them rulers of the works of your hands and you put everything under their feet." When God made Adam and Eve, he created them with glory and honor and gave them dominion to rule the earth. Given dominion over God's creation. Crowned with glory and honor. Here's where our story begins. But a fall came, which we will discuss later on.

When God created you, he marked you with glory and honor, and when you received Christ, you received Christ in you-- the hope of glory. (If you are reading this book and have not made a decision to receive Christ as your Savior, then you will get an opportunity to read about this and receive him or be "born again" at the end of Chapter 1.) So when you received Christ, You became a carrier of God's glory—a container filled with glory. In Rev. 3:11, it says, "I am coming soon. Hold on to what you have, so that no one will take your crown." From the time we are created in Father's heart, the enemy begins to try to steal our crown. Before conception, in the womb, during birth, and thereafter. When God began to download revelation for this book, he brought to my own memory of a trauma event that I had not recalled. I was 9 years old and I would be in the courtyard of my elementary school for recess and I had a girl and a pack of girls that would run up behind me and take my hat off all the while calling me names and then the girls would surround me and play catch with my hat. I would either chase them to get it back or I would stand there and just cry while they called me names and say word curses and intimidating labels on me. This is a picture of how we as Christians are taunted by the world, the flesh and the devil. Regularly, someone is trying to steal our crown of glory and honor that we already have in Jesus. That is why Rev. 3:11, in the KJV says, "Let no one "steal" your crown. Not borrow, or take. It is illegal for the enemy to steal our crown and he can only take what we allow him to take. The "head" also refers symbolically to the place of authority. When we were created with glory and honor, through the fall, we lost it, and then Jesus died on the cross and went and got our glory and honor back for us.

The goal of this book is to define the Ichabod Curse, look at how this curse manifests in the life of a believer, particularly in the shroud of shame, and to look at how the life of Jesus and the Bible gives us keys and strategies and examples of how to break the Ichabod Curse off of our lives, once and for all be delivered from the lies, and to walk in true freedom.

In my years as a counselor, I have seen this curse manifest in so many ways in the lives of amazing men and women, who just want to simply serve God with their lives and live in the joy of their salvation. So throughout these chapters, I will be using real life case studies that many of us can relate to, and the way the Holy Spirit revealed the keys to break these men and women free of their bondage. In every case, I believe that there is a root curse that keeps these people bound, and I am using this book to expose how this root curse manifests and what every one of us can do about it. I have always said that if you don't know your options, you have none. This book is giving you options to long standing toxic roots, broken relationships, and being satisfied with just living a half-life, versus the life Jesus died to give you.

In each chapter, I also release a prophetic word given by God in that particular session pertaining to that issue, so that as you are reading these words, the word of the Lord—the truth—can be released over your issue and shift you from darkness to light; from lies to the truth of how God sees you and your particular problem.

At the end of each chapter, I also give you a prayer of deliverance and decrees to make over your life. You can pray these prayers by yourself. Because of the ministry of the Holy Spirit, you don't need a human being there to pray these over yourself. When you pray in the Name of Jesus, you have Jesus, Father God, and the Holy Spirit there with you praying. Yourself + 3 = Four. So when you pray, you actually have four altogether. Isaiah 10:27 says, "He will break the yoke of slavery and lift if from their shoulders....from off their neck, and the yoke shall be destroyed because of the anointing." So I always say that:
THE ANOINTING + ANYTHING = EVERYTHING. You are not alone as you go through the deliverance in this book—you have the greatest power in heaven and earth ready to destroy all the crapdom that the world, the flesh and the devil has tried to destroy you with.

CHAPTER ONE

THE FIRST SIGHTINGS OF THE ICHABOD CURSE

"You shall not surely die", the serpent said to the woman. "For God knows that when you eat of it your eyes will be opened and you will be like God, knowing good and evil." –Genesis 3: 4-5

The case study we will look at is that of Satan, and that of Adam and Eve, and their father, named God. The original curse of the glory connection of humanity to God was in the Garden.

Adam and Eve were the first married couple that we see in the Bible. They were also the first humans created. So, there they are, in a beautiful place called Eden, with all kinds of trees that were pleasing to the eye, good food, and what felt like all the time in the world. Just the two of them and God. They were just enjoying God and his glory. God was happy because he created them so he could have some humans to hang out with and fellowship with. He created them because he wanted a family he could have relationship with. He created you because he wanted you in his family.

God, being the great protector of the family that he is, told Adam and Eve that they could eat of any of the trees, except for the Tree of the Knowledge of Good and Evil. So he planted the Tree of Life and The Tree of the Knowledge of Good and Evil in the middle of the Garden of Eden, where they lived. This is important because he gave them the free will to choose what tree they would eat from. This also tells us that evil was already present at this time.

So one day, Eve was going to pick out fruit for her and Adam, and Satan, in the form of a serpent, came and asked her, "Did God really say: You must not eat from every tree in the garden"? So she replied, "God said that we must not touch that tree or we will die."

I'll get back to this cliffhanger in a minute. But I have to ask, "Have you ever been in a really blessed season of your life, and all of a sudden, someone comes in and casts doubt and negativity on your blessing and starts to suck out all of your joy?"

Well, I call these people "joy suckers". Many times, these joy suckers come to spew their death words on you because they are miserable and they won't be happy until you are miserable also. They will come and cast doubt on what God has already told you to be true. They have already made a choice in their own lives that has caused the glory of God to depart, and they want company for their trip to Doom and Gloom-Ville. Well, this is exactly what happened to Eve. Satan, named Lucifer in Isaiah 14, was the head worshipping angel. He was very beautiful and filled with the glory of the Lord. In fact, his original name Lucifer means, "brightness". Isaiah 14: 12-14, God is talking and he says, "How you are fallen from heaven, O Day Star, son of Dawn! How you are cut down to the ground, you who laid the nations low! You said in your heart, "I will ascend to heaven; I will raise my throne above the stars of God: I will sit on the mount of assembly on the heights of Zaphron: I will ascend to the tops of the clouds, I will make myself like the Most High". So, Lucifer had a destiny from God, and instead of being part of the family of God, he decided he wanted to rebel and do his own thing—and take all the glory from God, and use the inheritance to have a hostile takeover of God and his company. So in Ezekiel 28, we find a very clear description of Satan and he is described as the anointed cherub.

Whenever anything created by God decides that they will reject their God-given destiny, they will have to settle for a counterfeit. So when we do it God's way, we get God's results. When we do it our way, we get our results.

So we see that Satan, had already made a choice that caused his butt to be kicked out of heaven and for the glory to depart from him. So when Satan fell like lightning from heaven, he took one-third of the angels with him and that wasn't enough, so he wanted to start to try to lie to humans and get them to keep him company in his pathetic state.

Okay, we're back. So then Satan deceives Eve and Adam to touch and eat of the Tree of the Knowledge of good and evil, and as soon as they do, they are aware of evil, and when God finds them, Adam says, "I heard you in the garden, and I was afraid because I was naked, so I hid." So the Lord releases the consequence for their actions of disobedience. The Lord didn't send the curse—the actions that they sowed reaped a consequence of spiritual death. In other words, the original glory had departed and now the glory was tainted.

So we see this pattern of Satan, because he was already kicked out of heaven, all that glory departed, and ever since, He has been coming to deceive others to get in to pride so the glory leaves them also. Or He convinces faithful Christians, through lies, that the glory of God has also departed from them. So they spend the rest of their lives outside the glory of God here on the earth and in eternity. WHEN YOU BELIEVE THE LIE, YOU EMPOWER THE LIAR!! WHEN YOU BELIEVE THE TRUTH, YOU EMPOWER THE SPIRIT OF TRUTH IN YOU, WHICH IS THE HOLY SPIRIT!

So what is the good news here? God didn't want to leave humanity like that, so he provided a sacrifice —a once for all—sacrifice to take all of our sins. This sacrifice is Jesus Christ. He willingly chose to go to a cross, die for you and I, and then he rose from the dead. He nailed every sin we ever committed, are committing, or will commit, to the cross. So when we confess our sins, and believe on Jesus Christ, and make him Lord over our lives, the original glory that was given away, in the Garden, all comes back for us. When he did this, he went down into hell and got the keys out of Satan's hands—the keys of death, hell, and the grave. Satan thought he won—he thought that he had us in a perpetual state of living out the Curse of Ichabod—but really, God had a plan to redeem our lives back so we could live in the original glory he always had for us. How do I know this? I'm glad you asked. Even in the middle of our mess, Christ decided that we were valuable enough to die for.

Romans 3:23, "for all have sinned and come short of the glory of God." So none of us, apart from receiving Jesus as our Lord, have any glory or righteousness. Romans 6:23- "For the wages of sin is death, but the gift of God is eternal life in Christ Jesus, our Lord." So this is a free gift for all—no extra charge. Why would God do this for us? Cause we are his family that he created and he wants the best for us. He is a very loving father. Romans 5:8 says, "But God demonstrated his own love toward us, that while we were still sinners, Christ died for us." God did this for you because of his great love for you. You might be saying, I don't want to live this life with the glory departed from my life—but how do I get that back? What do I have to do to have eternal life with God and guarantee that my life is protected everyday with the honor and glory that God promises? Romans 10:9-10 says, "that if you confess with your mouth the Lord Jesus and believe in your heart that God has raised Him from the dead, you will be saved. For with the heart one believes unto righteousness and with the mouth confession is made unto salvation." If you want to guarantee that you are positioned for all of God's blessing in your life, here on earth, as well as in the life to come for eternity, then do the following three steps:

1. Read out loud the "Prophetic Word Concerning Salvation" so you can internalize Father God's heart toward you.
2. Read out loud the "Salvation Prayer"

3. Read the "Decree a Thing" section aloud for the next 21 days and/or anytime you feel yourself doubting your salvation in God. Why read aloud? Because when you speak, your promises are voice-activated to your own spirit, the world around you and the devil. This empowers the authority you have to reinforce what God has promised. This also brings God in remembrance of what he has promised is yours in Christ Jesus.

PROPHETIC WORD CONCERNING SALVATION

"For I say unto you this day: the justice of man is trying to hang you, but my mercy is there to cut the rope. You will not die by the lies and deceptions and schemes of man and the enemy of your soul. But you will live, and not die to declare the glory of your Lord in the land of the living. For I say unto you—I will judge the quick and the dead. My mercy will triumph over any judgment of man, the enemy, and your own soul. In just the nick of time, as the justice of man has come to hang you, my mercy is coming to cut the rope. Where you were ready to take your last breath, I sent the Ruach of my Spirit in, and you will breathe easily once again. I say unto you again, "What ropes are around your neck—trying to hang you? Whose words are strangling the life out of you?" I am sending my archangels right now, today, with swords I have put in their hands, to cut the ropes around your neck. For, because of my son,

Jesus, justice would have hung you, but my mercy, cut the ropes. I am cutting the ropes off of you neck right today. Rise above your own confession and allow my words to free you and live."

SALVATION PRAYER

Heavenly Father, I confess that I am a sinner, who has been living without the glory that Jesus brought back for me on the cross. I confess that I need you, Jesus. Please forgive me of my sins, come into my heart. Be my Lord and Savior, and fill me with the Holy Spirit, to guide me and teach me in all my ways." Thank you, Jesus, for making a way for me to get back to my glory and honor status.
In Jesus Name,
Amen

DECREE A THING

- I decree that I have a glorious future in Christ.
- I decree that I am full of hope when I think about my future.
- I belong to the eternal kingdom of God, which will never be shaken.
- The Lord protects me from all evil, all my days.
- God sets a banquet before me in the presence of my enemies.
- Goodness and mercy follow me all the days of my life.
- No weapon formed against me shall prosper.

- God works everything together for my good in every situation in life. I am a winner!
- I am steadfast in the Lord, immovable, secure in His blessings.
- God's glorious favor over my life fills all my days and is a shield around me, protecting me from evil.

Decrees based on the following scriptures: Jeremiah 29:11, Hebrews 12:28, Psalm 121:7, Psalm 23:5-6, Isaiah 54:17, Romans 8:28, I Corinthians 15:58, Psalm 5:1

CHAPTER TWO

THE NAMING OF ICHABOD: GETTING TO THE ROOT, NOT JUST THE FRUIT

**"As she was dying, the women attending her said, "Don't despair, you have given birth to a son. But she did not respond or pay any attention. She named the boy Ichabod, saying, 'The glory has departed from Israel." –
I Samuel 4:20-21**

As I went into prayer and the court of the Lord to present my cases for the day, I brought the name of John, one of my clients, that would be coming in for a session, with his wife, Julia, later on that day. John is a man him most of his life, emasculated him through unrighteous control and manipulation, and punished him for the abandonment of her husband, his father.

He struggles with road rage, outbursts of anger, and an ongoing addiction with pornography and lust. He is a Christian man, loves his wife and his son, but has been seeing the childhood patterns he lived through beginning to manifest in his own son. He desperately wants to be close to his teenage son, but finds himself in unrighteous arguments and fits of rage with him. His wife, because of this pattern, has stepped up and done some things to deal with the fruit, so as just to keep the peace in the family, which is always short-term.

As I presented John's name, the Lord led me to I Samuel 4. The spiritual climate of this chapter, and the judge and spiritual priest over Israel, Eli, and his death, marked the end of the dark period of the judges when most of the nation ignored God. As I began to read through the text, It was basically a story of how the Philistines, the enemy of Israel, not only defeated, in a day, 30,000 foot soldiers in a battle, but how, a prophecy about Eli's sons, Hophni and Phineas, who were not living for God, would be killed, and in fact, were killed in this battle. The arc of the covenant, which symbolized God's presence and power, was taken from the Israelites by their enemy, the Philistines. So the belief of the Israelites was that when the ark was captured by their enemies, that Israel's glory was gone and that God has deserted them. The great defeat of that battle that day came because they were turning the ark into idol worship, over honoring their relationship with God by doing his commands. So the atmosphere of this chapter is one of death, dying, glory leaving, defeat, and darkness.

As I read the chapter before it, I learned that the Lord told Samuel that he was about to judge Eli's family because of the sin Eli knew about his two sons, who made themselves contemptible; and he failed to restrain them. What this tells us is that Eli failed to discipline his sons. As I was reading these chapters, the Lord began to give me a word of strategy—a key to healing for my client John. He said, "Break the curse of Ichabod off of John." And I said, I don't know what the curse of Ichabod is. Then he led me to I

Samuel 4:19-21, and I began to connect the prophetic dots.

In these passages, it says: **"Eli's daughter-in-law, the wife of Phineas, was pregnant and near the time of delivery. When she heard the news that the ark of God had been captured and that her father-in-law and her husband were dead, she went into labor and gave birth, but was overcome by her labor pains. As she was dying, the women attending her said, 'Don't despair; you have given birth to a son.' But she did not respond or pay any attention."**

I believe that the curse of Ichabod is one where the glory of God has departed off of a life because of the sins of the father being passed down the bloodline which results in rebellion or a belief system that the glory of God has departed off of one's life and that life is lived just responding to that curse. How does this happen? I believe it happens through fatherlessness. Eli, I believe represents fatherlessness, and Hophni and Phineas represent the orphans that were born out of a lack of true relationship, discipline, and loving correction that comes with the spirit of sonship. I believe that Eli's daughter-in-law represents each one of us in this season, pregnant with a promise, and the women attending to her represent the voice of the Lord telling her that out of the rubble of the generational sins of his father, that new life has been born. These women told her not to despair, and to focus on what she had given birth to. Instead of blessing him, the baby, with a name that represents new life and a new chance and a new expectation for a new tomorrow, she prophecies the gloom and doom of the atmosphere around her over her son, naming him Ichabod, which means "the glory of the Lord has departed". Then she dies leaving him as an orphan, with no parents. The account also tells us that when the women gave her an encouraging word, she didn't pay attention to the word from them.

So this begs the question for you and I. Are we allowing the culture of death and the fear around us to affect the atmosphere of glory we already carry in the person of Jesus Christ or are we allowing the glory within us, and what we are birthing to change the atmosphere around us? What is coming out of us has the power to change everything around us. Jesus' natural birth surroundings and atmosphere never altered his identity or his personal destiny! The fact is that he had a death decree in his land, ready to give a legal right to kill him if he was found. The fact that he was born in a lowly stable and humble estate never caused him to live a lowly belief system about why he was created. Both Mary and Joseph had to heed the words of the Lord in order for the details surrounding Jesus' birth and thereafter, to go forth and be accomplished. They did not allow the fear of Herod to fill their hearts so that they pushed that fear off on Jesus; but they allowed Herod's behavior to propel them to protect and secure Jesus' destiny and future even more!!! Herod's reign of terror and the atmosphere created by it was not the object they allowed as an excuse to give up and shut down the great plan God had for their son. On the contrary,

Herod's reign of terror was a greater confirmation of the greatness that their child was destined for. WHEN DEMONS ARE ANNOYING YOU, THEY ARE CONFIRMING YOU!!!!

Jesus was birthmarked for glory and honor. Ichabod was birth marked for glory and honor, but his mother chose to allow the oppression that surrounded his birth to mark his life by labeling him Ichabod—which prophesied, "the glory of God has departed off of your life." And so it is with us. I submit to you that each one of us are living and responding out of one of these camps. We are either living out of the camp marked, from birth, for glory and honor, knowing we are honored by our Heavenly Father and marked for greatness or we are living out of the camp of "Ichabod", where the world, the flesh, or the devil has convinced us that the glory of God has departed from us and there is not a place for us in Father God's heart or the heart of others. In this present season, it will be difficult for many to worship and give honor to the Lord, receive new mantles, and release others into their God-given birthrights, unless we realize something important. You cannot give away what you don't believe you possess in the first place and you can't possess it if you do not believe you were marked for it or worthy of it! You can quote scriptures as long as the day is long about how Christ became sin for us and how we carry his glory, but if you don't believe it, no one else in your sphere of influence will believe it either. This curse of Ichabod has so many Christians bound up in epidemic proportions and I submit to you that you cannot conquer what you don't confront. As we go through the many ways that this curse manifests, ask the Holy Spirit to show you where that is showing up in your life, your thinking, your relationships and your choices. Then pray the yoke-destroying deliverance prayers at the end of each chapter.

Many times, our identity is created by our parents' lens of the natural atmosphere surrounding our birth versus the spiritual atmosphere of heaven—where our real identity originated. Instead of tapping into that, parents tap into their own limited understanding of the natural atmosphere surrounding the birth of their child and instead of speaking God's truth over that child to establish them in blessings, they are now labeled and named something that reflects the culture and limits them to a lifelong identity crisis. But this goes even deeper.

In Exodus 20:4 -6, the Lord tells Israel, "You shall not make for yourself an idol in the form of anything in heaven above or on the earth beneath or in the waters below. You shall not bow down to them or worship them; for I, the Lord your God, am a jealous God, punishing the children for the sin of the fathers to the third and fourth generation of those who hate me, but showing love to a thousand generations those who love me and keep my commandments." I submit to you, that, these commandments were not given to show how perfect we could be—but to show how much in need of a Savior—Jesus—we actually are. When the sins and curses coming down a family line are alcoholism, drugs, or sexual abuse, the problem is easily identified. With so called "less serious sins", the source of the problem is usually not even identified as generational. People simply explain it away by concluding, "Oh, he's just like his father, and you know what he was like."

God sees man in terms of families. He thinks in terms of generations. How often do we see in scripture: "I am the God of Abraham, Issac, and Jacob." So the bad news is that we are affected by our parents' sins. The good news is that God has provided the way for our freedom from all the effects of their iniquity. What God requires, God provides. **In Leviticus 26:40-42, God gives us a pattern and a promise for freedom. If we confess our sins and the sins of our fathers, and we humble ourselves, He will remember His covenant. That is, He remembers that we are part of His family. This is called IDENTIFICATIONAL REPENTANCE because we identify with our ancestors and repent on their behalf, as well as our own. This breaks the power of the pressure of sins of the fathers and the resulting curses. Excellent examples of this in the Bible are found in Daniel 9, Ezra 9, Nehemiah 2 and 9.**

Confession and repentance are God's provision for us: **1 John 1:9 says, "If we confess our sins, he is faithful and just to forgive us our sins and to cleanse us from all unrighteousness."(KJV)**

It's not enough to deal with the fruit of the Ichabod curse. It is important to look for the root or roots. Look at this example of Jesus' earthly ministry in Mark 9:17, which says, "A man in the crowd comes up to Jesus and says, "Teacher, I brought you my son, who is possessed by a spirit that has robbed him of speech. Whenever it seizes him, it throws him to the ground. He foams at the mouth, gnashes his teeth and becomes rigid (rebellious). I asked the disciples to drive out the spirit, but they could not." Then in verse 19, Jesus says, "Oh, you unbelieving generation, how long shall I stay with you? How long shall I put up with you? Bring the boy to me." So in verse 20, they bring the boy to Jesus and it says that when the spirit saw Jesus, it immediately threw the boy into a convulsion. He fell to the ground and rolled around, foaming at the mouth." Now, you would think Jesus would just say the word and heal him, right? Wrong. Jesus turns to the boy's father and says, "How long had the boy been like this"? This is what we call counseling intake—Jesus is looking to see where the roots of this condition started with the boy. The father says, "From childhood. It has often thrown him in for fire or water to kill him. But if you can do anything, take pity on us and help us." Jesus replies back, 'If you can'? "Everything is possible for him who believes."

What was Jesus doing here? He was identifying the generational spirit of unbelief or spirit of slumber. Out of the father's mouth, he says, "I believe, but please help my unbelief." So in this verse 24, the root spirit that opened the door for this spirit that was tormenting this boy was identified. I believe the father's admittance of need to help with his unbelief was repentance and repentance always proceeds deliverance. In verse 25, Jesus says, "You deaf and mute spirit, I command you, come out of him and never enter him again." This text shows us that these "sins of the father", as they are called in the book of Exodus, are generational and will continue down the bloodline if they are not taken care of.

So, getting back to our client John. In that session, many of the lies he was believing about himself and the Curse of Ichabod-his belief that he wasn't worthy and that he had to control everything in his environment in order to control the places where pain could come from-was exposed and dealt with. What was the work we needed to do in this session? The first thing we did was diffusing some of the triggering mechanisms to break his pull towards a false intimacy with the pornography addiction; this is a trauma tool that I use. This trauma tool is not in this book. A future book will be published for healing trauma. We did some additional work with memories to achieve trauma resolution. But before any of that, we had to begin to deal with helping him come out of agreement with the lies that he was believing about himself. That is why this book was written, to explain the lies, and what to do with them, once they are exposed.

Doing this helped him gain freedom and put him on the road to recovery and walking in the knowledge of the fact that he was birthmarked by God for glory and honor. We also helped him to deal with forgiving his parents, his own repentance for his ungodly response to his parents' behavior, and also used decrees of the truth to replace the lies with the truth. If you see yourself in this chapter, and you know, that at a core level, that someone or something has stolen your crown of glory and honor, either through word curses your parents spoke over you when you were growing up, or authority figures in your life; or if you feel that you just never fit in, have always felt like an outcast, not belonging, or not belonging in the presence or the house of God, as in church, then you may have this curse as a root attached to your true identity.

So, now that you realize that you were marked from birth with glory and honor, and you see that you have been believing the lie that you are not qualified for glory and honor or a lifestyle of receiving the good things that God has for you, what can you do? I am glad you asked. It is a three step process:

1. Read out loud the prophetic word below. As you do, the atmosphere of hopelessness around you will dissolve, and hope will rise as you hear the truth of God's heart for you, as well as how he sees and feels about you.

2. Pray "The Prayer of Renunciation of the Ichabod Curse" out loud one time. By doing this, you are disengaging with the lies and empowering the truth. You are detaching yourself from the liar and attaching yourself to the truth giver—the Lord. You are also God's representative closing access points in your family history where these doors were opened. So you are cleansing the family pipeline for yourself, your children, the past sins, and replacing it with a blessing of God that will go forward to a thousand generations.

3. Make the decrees listed under "DECREE A THING" section of this chapter out loud. Do this for the next 30 days. Job 22:28 says, "Thou shalt decree a thing, and it shall be established unto thee, and the light shall shine upon thy ways." Doing this will cause the negative belief pattern to break and for the truth of God's word and the good plan he has promised you in his word, to be established.

4. The last thing you need to do, after doing steps 1-3, is to close your eyes, lift your hands up, and say, "Heavenly Father, now that I have handed you some of the hurt of my past, what do you have for me in exchange"? Just sit there for a few minutes, and you may see, sense, or hear something. God is always speaking to us if we pay attention and get silent long enough to listen. You may hear a word or see an image, or you may just sense God's peace that wasn't there before you did these steps to freedom. Whatever happens, write it down in your journal as a reminder that you can hear God for yourself and the more you do this, the more you will want to begin to commune with God this way, and hear what he might say personally to you.

PROPHETIC WORD
The Word of the Lord says:

"You are focused on building your house, but I say, I am focused on building your temple. I long to build my home inside of you. For I have said in my word, "Heaven is my throne and the earth is my footstool—where is the house you build for me? I desire to do a reconstruct of your heart and your dwelling place—so I can reside with you and in you. You are my child, and I desire happy, joy-filled times with you. If you call to me and invite me into your day, you and I will build your temple together and the desecration from false fathers will be a thing of the past and the glory of the latter house will be greater than the glory of the former house.

I honor you, my child, as you honor me. You are precious to me and I need you to help me build my Kingdom on earth. It is not a natural kingdom built with earthly hands, but one built on the incorruptible seed of my Son, Jesus. He is the firm foundation and the chief cornerstone. As you go through your days, look over your shoulder, and I will be right there next to you, causing your heart to embrace my love and walk in my love—even concerning those things you don't understand. All the schemes of hell and the plans of man; nor time can change what I hold for you in my heart. You don't have to fix it all in a day.

We will fix it together and build the dream I have always had in my heart for you—together. You are not alone. I love you. I embrace you. I am proud to claim you as my own, beloved child.

Don't' forget these words that I tell you. For as we rebuild your temple, the enemies you see before you, you will see no more. You're a winner because you have chosen the winning side and I am your champion cheering you on to higher heights and greater victory. Know that I will never give up on you. I love you with an everlasting love that knows no bounds. I am the family you seek, I am your all in all and I know that I will never leave you nor forsake you. We will build it together and your enemies will be a thing of the past—rendered powerless forever.

What we build together based on my Word, will be the plumb line by which all your relationships are measured. It's a new standard, a new day, a new way. I am bringing you up to code for the destiny I have for you and I won't leave this undone. Stay close to me, hear my word and obey it, and you will bring many sons and daughters to my glory."

PRAYER OF RENUNCATION OF THE ICHABOD CURSE

Heavenly Father, on behalf of myself and my family line, I renounce and repent for all generational fatherlessness that led to the Ichabod Curse on me and my family line. I forgive my earthly father for _____ (take a minute and name those hurts, for the purpose of letting them go off of you and onto Jesus), and for misrepresenting you to me by not being present, and for not meeting the needs of protection, security, and identity. Lord, forgive me for every way that I have disqualified myself to walk in the life that Jesus died to give me. I also forgive my mother for

_____ (take a

minute to name those hurts, for the purpose of letting them go off of you and onto Jesus).

Lord, I ask you to help me forgive everyone who I looked to as a spiritual father or leader who wounded and failed me, or abused or misused me. Lord, I release all hatred, bitterness, and revenge over to you now. I know he hurt me because someone hurt him, and I release him now over to you. I break agreement with demons and any unholy alliances holding lies in place about him. I send all spirits of rejection, hatred, shame, and condemnation back to the feet of Jesus now. Lord, please forgive me for the negative heart expectation that I have that says that anyone in my life that represents a spiritual father will, in fact, hurt me the same way or that you, Lord, will hurt me because my earthly father did.

I speak to the poverty spirit to leave me now, in Jesus Name. I renounce all lack, fear of lack and ungodly control because of fear of lack. I ask you to release blessings in its place right now, and I call back any portion of my spirit that has rejected life because of the Ichabod Curse. I bind my body, heart and spirit to God's will and purpose for me. Lord, I ask that you would heal my mind and my heart from spirits of abandonment, rejection, and fatherlessness. I ask you to release the Zoe of God over me right now and saturate my spirit, soul, body, memory, will and processing.

God, please help me to have the heart of a son/ daughter and please help me to turn my heart towards you, Father, and a spiritual father in the faith. Lord, I ask that you would direct someone in to my life that will represent you well, to me, as a spiritual father, Lord. Help me to know this person by the spirit, and when I do, help me to commit to them and to a church family. Father, raise me in the power of your love, so that I may bring others along in to their birthright and destiny, for your Kingdom. Father, would you now supernaturally remove all unrighteous birthmarks from my spirit that are not of you? Please remove all unrighteous motives, struggling, and control from my spirit that is activated in me when I feel dishonored, ignored, invisible, or rejected. Replace these unrighteous birthmarks with an automatic response to look to your truth of love for me, whenever the world around me rejects who you made me to be or when the storms or seasons of life pull away support systems I have depended on for my security. In Jesus Name, Amen.

DECREE A THING

- I decree that God loves me with an everlasting love and an unfailing kindness.

- I decree that I was wonderfully and fearfully made by God and that I am not a mistake.
- I decree that when I am brokenhearted, that God is very close to me to comfort me.
- I decree that nothing can separate me from the love of God.
- I decree that neither death, nor life, nor angels, nor demons, neither mu fears for today or my worries about tomorrow, the powers of hell or the power in the sky above or in the earth below, can separate me from the love of my Father, God.
- I decree that God rejoiced over me on the day of my birth, and rejoices over me with singing.
- I decree that I am worthy of your love, Lord, and the love of others.
- I decree that I am the head and not the tail, that I am wanted, cherished, and was completely expected by you and timed by Your Divine hand, Lord.
- I decree that I embrace the truth that I always have a home in your arms and in your heart, Daddy God.
- I embrace the truth that what You say about me trumps what broken man or women says about me.
- I decree that you Father, will never leave me or forsake me.

The scripture used in these decrees are: Romans 8, 31-39, Zephaniah 3:17, Deuteronomy 28:13,

Jeremiah 21:3, Psalm 139, Psalm 34:18, Deuteronomy 31:8, and Hebrews 13:5.

PROPHETIC ACTIVATION

- Close your eyes.
- Lift up your hands
- Say, "Heavenly Father, as I have handed you the lies from the Ichabod Curse, What do you have for me in exchange?"
- Wait for a few minutes and discern if you see, hear, or sense something.
- Write down anything you see, hear or sense in your journal.
- If you do not see, hear, or sense something, just be patient with yourself.
- Discernment happens by reason of use, through the senses. The more you practice expecting to hear from the Lord, the sharper your discernment gift will be. Hebrews 5:14 says, "But solid food is for the mature, who by constant use have trained themselves to distinguish good from evil."

CHAPTER THREE

THE ICHABOD CURSE MANIFESTING AS CONDEMNATION

"No weapon that is formed against you shall prosper,
and every tongue that rises up against you in
judgment will be condemned."

-Isaiah 54:17

As the woman entered my counseling office, I could see the shroud Of shame over her face. She had a black veil over her face and a weight—like the old stocks that prisoners would be placed in when in prison—over her shoulder. As I opened up in prayer, I discerned a heavy spirit of self-condemnation on her. This woman had a stronghold of lesbianism. When she moved to New York years ago, she began to get counseled from a woman pastor in a church that she trusted. The counselor took advantage of her vulnerability and exploited this woman's trust by subtly inviting her into a lesbian relationship with her. After a time, she renounced that life and moved out of NY City; however, any where she went, women with the same spirit would attach to her and invite her into this lifestyle. She was convinced—even though she has been married to a man for 15 years, that she still had a door open to lesbianism—the unnatural affection of a woman to a woman. But as I sat there and released this prophetic word over her, the Lord allowed her to see that it wasn't that lesbian spirit at all---she had received deliverance for that prior to coming to see me for a session. No, it was something else—even more subtle.

In the prophetic word God gave me pertaining to this, I sense God saying the following: **"You sing and say, 'How great is our God'. But I ask, "How great is your God"? I birthed something out of nothing and I hold the world in space. I poured forth a grace that is greater than all your sin", says the Lord. Are you greater than me?", says the Lord. For I say unto you, "I have already forgiven you—but you do not forgive yourself. If I forgave you, in all of my greatness and majesty, than why will you not forgive yourself? It is not enough to forgive your perpetrator and offender, you must forgive yourself and when you do, you humble your greatness under my greater greatness, and as you do this, you will be free and my glory will flow through you and out of you everywhere you place your foot. I am the Lord and there is no other."**

When we do not release ourselves from our own mistakes, mishaps, and hang- ups, and times that we have missed the mark, then, in that moment, we are saying, "we are greater than God and our opinion has a higher place than his. We actually "frustrate the love and the grace of God". **In Galatians 2:21, Paul says, "I do not frustrate the grace of God; for if righteousness comes by the law, then Christ is dead in vain."** Did you realize that you have the power to frustrate God and his grace and love in your life? Why? Because God is saying "I have already forgiven you, but you won't forgive yourself—so are you greater than me? And when we say that and believe that, and live our lives based on that lie, we stay lodged in that condition—the enemy will keep on shaming us and God's hands are tied because we, as an act of our will are saying, "My opinion of me trumps what God says and is greater than his. My opinion is that I am unforgiveable, but in Hebrews 8:12, God says, **"I will forgive their wickedness and will remember their sins no more."** When we say, "What I did is unforgiveable, --then it is." How do I know this? **Proverbs 23:7 says, "For as a man thinketh in his heart, so is he."**

When we choose, as an act of our will, not to forgive ourselves, we are our own worst enemy. Why? Because out of judging ourselves, we actually condemn ourselves. How do I know this? I'm glad you asked. **Isaiah 54:17 tells us that "No weapon that is formed against us will prosper and every tongue that shall rise against your in judgment shall be condemned."** So therefore, according to this scripture, if you are judging yourself as not being worthy of being forgiven, than your own judgment of yourself is keeping you in condemnation. The enemy doesn't have to do anything—you have already guaranteed that you will live in a constant state of being condemned by yourself and the enemy.

John 10:10 says, "The thief comes only to kill, steal, and destroy, but I have come that they may have life and have it to the full." When we bring judgment on ourselves by coming into agreement with the condemnation of the enemy—then the enemy has our own agreement that we are condemned.

What is the good news? **I John 3:20 says, "Though my heart condemns me, God is greater than my heart." Romans 8:1 says, "Therefore there is no condemnation to them that are in Christ Jesus, who walk not after the flesh, but after the Spirit. For the law of the Spirit of life in Christ Jesus hath made me free from the law of sin and death."** We can, as an act of our will, not a feeling, choose to forgive ourselves for that past sin, hang up, mistake, etc., and choose to walk out of the enemy's camp today and back into the "No Condemnation Zone" that Christ gave to us through his finished work on the cross. We do this by repenting for judging ourselves contrary to what the Word of God says, and thereby, taking ourselves out of the path of the destroyer.

It is difficult to talk about condemnation without bringing up the fear issue. I am going to give you three passages to understand why the enemy of your soul—Satan, and his minions, has had such a focus in the area of fear. When we understand why he has made it a priority of promoting fear, then it will help us to have the resolve to be insulated from things that we have been vulnerable to.

Isaiah 51:12, "I, even, I, am He that comforts you. Who are you that you should be afraid of a man who will die and forget the Lord your maker? He stretched out the heavens and made the foundations of the earth—and yet you feared continually every day." In this verse, God is standing before us saying, "I'm the one who stands before you, have you noticed my size? Have you forgotten that I can squash your enemies like a bug in a New York minute?" It is like we are putting someone else's opinion of us in the place of God and making them God in our lives. I have heard it said that "opinions are like arm pits. Everybody has them, and some of them really stink!" Sometimes we need this jar into reality to remind us that when we choose fear, we are choosing the inferior over the absolute manifested presence of God who is here to defend me in any and every situation.

Secondly, **Isaiah 54:13 says, "All or your children will be taught by the lord, and great shall be the peace of your children." Then verse 14 says, "And righteousness shall be established and you shall be far from oppression for you shall not fear."** Look at that phrase. You will be far from oppression. Why? Because you will not fear. What is oppression? Oppression is that moment where we make agreement with a lie and we allow the atmosphere of darkness to influence our beliefs and our values. It is actually a cloud of darkness that comes when we believe the lie. Fear, often times, does not start out as a spirit of fear. Sometimes it a simple emotion. We can work ourselves into fear without the devil. We don't need the devil to be stupid. So some sins we always think are spiritual, but often times they start out in the natural realm, meaning what is seen. An extreme example of this is in Galatians 5 actually refers to witchcraft as a sin that starts as a sin of the flesh. Here's this occultic, demonic, world swirling about a person involved in witchcraft. But the scripture says that is starts off as a sin of the flesh. Witchcraft, in its simplest form is the "I want to be in charge and control your environment.", so that a person stays in charge. It is the absence of trust in God and it starts as a sin of the flesh that becomes supernaturally empowered and eventually becomes demonic. It becomes a stronghold of the demonic. It basically places the person with a stronghold to say, "Come right into my mind devil, and use me to do your will in a particular situation." And that spirit of fear is only too happy to have access to you to do his work. Satan needs human beings to work through to get his work done.

So fear, often just starts as, "I got a bill in the mail that I didn't expect and I don't have the money for it and you start feeding that thing and pretty soon, in no time at all, you are just buried in fear, worry and anxiety. Then we get buried in that thing and it actually invites the spirit realm to come and reinforce it and becomes a much bigger battle than when we were just dealing with our own discipline. So fear will always keep us in a place of being, "Under condemnation" over something. Condemnation will keep you under in an oppressive, heavy state of mind. This is different than conviction. Conviction of the Holy Spirit comes to highlight something in your life that is going to lead you into a situation that is not your highest good. So the Holy Spirit will come and give you sand paper in your gut, to bring you to a place of looking at your choice, repent for it, and do it God's way, so that you are protected from the consequence of that situation. Condemnation comes to keep you under, in a low place and conviction comes to life you up out of that dark place.

Philippians 1:27 says, "Let your conduct be worthy of the Gospel of Christ—so that whether I come and see you or am absent, I hear of your affairs and you stand fast in one mind, striving together for the faith of the Gospel-not in any way, terrified by your adversaries-which is to them proof of perdition (proof of eternal judgment), but to you, salvation." When it says, "not in any way terrified by your adversaries, which is to them proof of eternal judgment", it is really saying something that we have to remember. Every time you and I are victorious over a fear issue, what is broadcast on the P.A. of hell or powers of darkness, is gloom and doom and absolute fear and judgment. The enemies will try to get us to fear so they don't have to think about what is coming for them. Every time we are victorious over the fear issue, all the powers of darkness come face to face with the fact that they are eternally doomed and there is no resolution for them. That is what the victory over fear does—it pronounces and announces and reminds what is coming their way. No wonder the powers of darkness work so hard to get us in fear. If they can do that, then they can dislocate our sense of effectiveness, but also dislocate their thinking about what they are facing. How amazing is that? As we read already in an earlier chapter, Satan already got his butt kicked out of heaven and lost his chance to live accepted by God. So the enemy is going to bring fear that brings torment over your mind, so his focus is enjoying seeing you in torment, so that he doesn't have to think about his own.

As far as the powers and principalities that work for his kingdom are concerned, the bible also addresses that very plainly. **I Corinthians 2:6-10 says, "Yet when I am among mature believers, I do speak with words of wisdom, but not the kind of wisdom that belongs to this world or to the rulers of this world, who are soon coming to nothing. No, the wisdom we speak of is the mystery of God, his plan that was previously hidden, even though he made it for our ultimate glory before the world began. But the rulers of this world had not understood it; if they had; they would not have crucified our glorious Lord."** It is easy to see that the rulers of this world, according to God, are eternal nothings that are going nowhere. God takes weapons of mass destruction that are formed against us and takes them to convert them into tools to build us and creates us into the devil's worst nightmare. Every place in your life that is bringing you the most fear and condemnation is actually proof of your next victory, because the devil wouldn't be coming against you so hard in that area with a crucifixion unless there was a resurrection on the other side of that. When Jesus was crucified, died, and buried, the devil was having a celebration, and on the third day, when he rose, the devil was kicking himself that he ever messed with Jesus, because, now, redemption came to the whole world through the devils plan to kill Jesus. So the devil played right into God's hand and God's plan for Jesus' life. No matter what it looked like in those 3 days during Jesus' death, he still had one more move—he had the power and so do you and I!!!!

So fear kills us. It messes us up in the worst possible way because it connects us to a lie that empowers the liar. So it begs the question, how would you treat a friend that lied to you as often as your fears do? At some point, we have to be stop being impressed by the size of our problem and our deliverance begins at the point that we are no longer impressed by the size of our problem. This is the challenge for every single one of us. I was finishing up the writing of this book during the summer of 2017, when all of the hurricanes in the U.S started, the first one being Hurricane Harvey that hit the state of Texas. Steve Hartman, an anchorman for CBS Evening News, went on the road to Texas, during the disaster, and used a very powerful 3-minute commentary to show that when Mother Nature is at its worst, human nature is at its best. To quote him, he said, "Right before this hurricane hit, the big story in the news was that America was at each other's throats over race, religion, immigration and politics and then Hurricane Harvey came and pounded us with perspective. When the roof over your head becomes the floor beneath your feet, no one cares about the color or creed of his rescuer. No one passes judgment because a hero's boat is too big, or his means is too meager. No one says, "Thanks for the rope, but I'd rather wait for someone more like me." "And later, when they find themselves on the end of a dump truck, with a soggy shirt on their backs, I am guessing no one ever says, "They are better than the person suffering next to them." A lot of people in Texas and Louisiana lost everything, but they are rich with perspective tonight and blessed with a priceless respect for their community. The volunteers risked and lost their lives in service to their neighbors. Most Americans are heroes just waiting for their moment, and we are just grateful for every last one of them." As Steve Hartman ended his report, he left us with a challenge, of "when the flood waters recede, will we still be able to love at these same record levels?" In this commentary, he gives us a remedy for fear.

I John 4: 17-20 says, "This is how love is made complete among us so that we will have confidence on the day of judgment. In this world we are like Jesus. There is no fear in love. But perfect love drives out fear, because fear has to do with punishment. The one who fears is not made perfect in love. We love because he first loved us. Whoever claims to love God yet hates a brother or sister is a liar. For whoever does not love their brother and sister, whom they have seen, cannot love God, whom they have not seen." What is he saying here? The whole point is that when we confess we have a spiritual experience in the unseen realm, it has to be measurable in the seen realm. How we treat the natural world illustrates what we are claiming to have happened in our own personal lives. It is easy to have half the equation of this settled in our thinking. The emphasis has been on making sure that I am in a place to receive that loving touch from God. Why? Because perfect love casts out all fear. This is only partially true because the word perfect their means, "complete". Love that has been made complete casts out all fear. When the writer of these verses goes on, he talks about us loving people. Meaning, I have to give in order to be complete.

This scripture compels us to serve somebody. In serving others, someone worse off than yourself, love will become practical when it is demonstrated. As we saw in the example of the commentary on Hurricane Harvey, America was in great fear before the storm hit.

After the storm, helping each other brought perfect, demonstrated, complete love, and let them know the reality that there is something greater than our fear—love that helps another person. Bravery is not the absence of fear, it is the knowledge that there is something greater than our fear. I call this "The Job Principle". Job had lost everything. He had every right to be bitter, isolate, and curse himself and God. In the book of Job, we are told in chapter 42, that Job's healing came while he was praying for his friends. So this is another instance where this strategy works to cast out fear. Many times, fear and condemnation will keep our focus on our own needs, and actually this practice will keep us going deeper into the black hole. I consistently suggest to my clients that struggle with depression, to get out there and find someone to help so that you can heal quicker.

I want to conclude by focusing on the client in the origin of this chapter. Once the client above acknowledged that the legal right the enemy had to taunt her and torment her with lesbian spirits came because of her unwillingness to forgive herself over those sins and relationships, she prayed this prayer and took herself out of the path of the destroyer. She also identificationally repented on behalf of her bloodline for these sins. We can pray this on behalf of our families and ancestry so that God will also forgive their sins and begin to draw them out of the fear of the enemy and into a life of seeing and shining in the original glory that God has always had for them.

If you feel that you are in a constant cycle of self-judgment, fear, and condemnation and can't get out of it, then do the next 3 steps:

1. Pray the prayer "Prayer to Remove Oneself Out of the Path of the Destroyer" out loud.
2. Place your hand over your own heart, and say, "I bless my spirit to come forward and to turn around and connect with God spirit to spirit and remember these promises from God. I bless my spirit to remember...." (and then just recite the blessings over your spirit out loud) Do these blessings over your spirit for the next 21 days. Don't spend another second on the enemy's path of destruction.
3. Decree aloud Romans 8:1: "There is therefore now no condemnation for those that are in Christ Jesus." Decree this every day for the next 30 days.

"Prayer to Remove Oneself from the Path of the Destroyer"
Apostle Kelly McCann
True Colors Ministry, International, Inc.
kmcdrawn2him@yahoo.com

On behalf of myself and my generational line, I renounce and repent for every unrighteous word, heart attitude, thought, and emotion that came into agreement with darkness and placed me on the paths of unrighteousness, the path of the Destroyer. I repent and renounce where I have not blessed those who have persecuted me and who have said all manner of evil against me falsely. I repent and renounce,, where I have spoken ungodly words out of anger, vengeance, malice, slander, pride, unforgiveness, bitterness, jealousy, envy, perfectionism, finger pointing, fault finding, a critical spirit, shame, condemnation, rejection, control, manipulation, domination, competition, hatred, fear of every kind, superiority, and every other unrighteous word.

And Father, where I have brought judgment upon myself because every tongue that rises against others or against my self is condemned, and I brought judgment on myself, Father forgive me for condemning myself and others. Where my own words of judgment of my ancestors have brought us into this captive place of condemnation, Lord forgive us. Lord, I release your blood over all of these words, thought, emotions and heart attitudes in myself and my line. I repent and renounce for all times I have walked in these sins as a child of God, thereby causing the righteous power of God to be used for ungodly purposes to place others in the depths or the ungodly grid into places of captivity. Lord please remove me and all of my ancestors from the ungodly grid, height, width, length and depths.

Father, please send the blood of Jesus from this day back through my generational line to Adam and cleanse the words, emotions, thoughts and attitudes and the unrighteous authority and power that was released from them. Lord, I break all consequences off of my line and all future generations for these sins. Father, I proclaim that out of the heart the mouth speaks and that my generational line has imprisoned our hearts in the ungodly depths because of our words and agreement with darkness. Lord please remove our hearts, minds, mouths, emotions, memories, including generational memory from this ungodly depth and restore them in righteousness. In Jesus Name. Amen

(Isaiah 54:17) – "No weapon formed against you shall prosper and every tongue that rises against you in judgment will be condemned."

(John 10:10) – "The thief comes only to kill, steal, and destroy. But I have come that they may have life and have it to the full."

(Psalms 17:4) – "Concerning the works of men, by the word of thy lips I have kept me from the paths of the destroyer."

I BLESS MY SPIRIT TO REMEMBER THAT........

- I am far more precious than jewels and my value is far above rubies and pearls.
- Strength and dignity are my clothing and my position is strong and secure.
- I open my mouth and speak skillful and godly wisdom.
- I look well to how things go in my household and the bread of idleness, gossip, discontentment and self-pity, I will not eat.
- I look unto Jesus, therefore, I am strong in the Lord and in the power of His Might.
- God is my Father and I am His precious child.
- There is therefore now NO CONDEMNATION in me because I am in Christ Jesus.
- I forget those things which are behind me.
- I lay aside very sin and weight which so easily entangles me.
- I press on toward the prize of the high calling in Christ Jesus.
- I speak life in every situation so that the power of my tongue blesses all those in my sphere of authority and influence.

CHAPTER FOUR

BREAKING OFF THE CURSE OF ICHABOD ON YOUR WORSHIP

"You are worthy, our Lord and God, to receive glory and honor and power; for you created all things, and by you and for your good pleasure they were created." -Revelation 4:11

Worshipping God is a lifestyle. We worship God when we obey him in all things pertaining to our life. Worship is an attitude of your heart towards God that says, "God, you are first, you get my undivided attention, loyalty, and devotion. Worship connects us spirit to spirit with God and is the door that opens to help us discern what is on our Father's heart. Every aspect of our life is worship to God. We are all worshipping something with our time, talent, and treasure; but I would like to focus on the expression of our worship to God through singing, music, the dance, and the ministry arts, and those expressions that are released through us from earth to heaven alone, and in corporate meeting settings. Many believe that the worship is their ability to play an instrument, sing, harmonize, dance, or wave flags. However, these are expressions of it. True worship is an attitude of our hearts toward God. Years ago, I wrote a song entitled, *"Don't Worship the Worship Instead of the King".* It was meant to be funny, but it really had a punch in the chorus. The chorus was as follows:

> **"Don't worship the worship; the perfect song in just the right key;**
>
> **Don't worship the worship; your perfect voice in harmony;**
>
> **Don't worship the worship; that song that depends just on you;**
>
> **Just lift up your voice, praise with all of your might—put all your focus on Jesus—and see what God will do!!!!**

The case study subject for this chapter is myself and many slices of my life where worshipping God kept my focus where it needed to be. Rev. 19:10 says the testimony of Jesus is the spirit of prophecy. If our Heavenly Father has a will for our lives and Jesus speaks it through his Word, and the Holy Spirit carries it out on earth as we cooperate with Him, then it make sense to me that our worship should all point ourselves and others to Jesus. This way we can get the Father's will on the earth, in our lives, and then do what he says. I believe that worship, done in spirit and in truth, opens the door so we can understand what is on God's heart and respond to it.

I want to open up with a story that I call, "The Night of the Hurricane". About ten years ago, my worship partner at the time, and myself were invited to join another worship team for their service to minister at their Sunday service. So the two of us arrived at the church to rehearse on a Tuesday evening. Well, the worship leader and the drummer were arguing over the tempo, off and on, for about an hour; the guitarist and one of the singers were speaking the truth in love, forcefully concerning their idea of the harmony for one particular song in the set list. Then, before we could even get through the first song, the worship leader announced that the rehearsal was over early because the governor had called a state of emergency due to an impending storm that was coming, and we all had to pack up and go home. The worship leader left the key with us to pack up and lock up because he had to get home. So everybody packed up and left, except for the two of us. We were going to do one song just to get in the flow of worship, because that "rehearsal" we just witnessed was so grieving to us.

So, up until that point, if I ever wanted to harmonize to a song, I had to plunk out the notes on the keyboard, sing the part one thousand times, and hope that I would remember it when the time came to minister in the service. I had been praying that God would supernaturally give me the gift of harmonizing, but up until this point, I had not seen that manifest.

As we began to play and sing "We Fall Down", I literally heard angels singing with us in the room where we were. So my friend, who was playing her guitar, said, "Kelly, you are harmonizing to this song." And I said, "I am"?? She said, "Yes, how are you doing that?" I said, "I hear angels singing, and I am following what I hear them singing." She said,

"Hmmm"... and went onto another song, and the same thing happened. Then she went onto another song, and the same thing happened. She would switch to another harmony part and I would harmonize to whatever she sang. As this was going on, the presence of God was so thick on the altar where we were rehearsing, that we would fall over in our respective places where we were standing on the altar, and I was down on the floor underneath my keyboard----just in the glory of God—and she was in the choir loft, laying back on a chair, with her guitar in her hand. Then I heard God say, "I'm not in the hurricane, I'm not in the earthquake, but I am in the still small voice. Worship me, listen to me, tune your heart to my heart, make room for me, and I will always fill up the space. So many want what I can do, but the true worshippers want me—and when I come, my glory comes, and when my glory comes, the death that is trying to kill my sons and daughters, is swallowed up in victory again and again and again." This word that came from the Lord bore witness with my spirit. I had always believed that about worship. Since I was dramatically saved at 12 years old, I had always saw worship that way.

But from the point of that time on the altar, and going forward, that perspective just deepened. What God said to me in that moment, was eternal and timeless---"Stop looking for another move of God—and look for the heart of the God who moves." The first perspective looks for the doings of God, and puts all the weight of the worship on what humans can do for God and the second perspective looks to be with

God, in close proximity. The desire for this close proximity brings the manifested, tangible presence and glory of God in a greater way.

I am thankful to God for my talents in music, but if I can be honest, I have found out that there is always someone better than you or worse than you where musical talents are concerned. Over time, God has freed me from the fear of man, because ministering to God is different than performing for man. I thought that I was in a place of total freedom in this area, until a few years ago, when I was asked to come and sing with another band for a very big, well-named deliverance minister's event. It was an honor to be part of this team for this meeting and I was really excited about the rehearsals. Well, as prophetic as this team of people were, there was also still a spirit of perfectionism and religion present in the rehearsals. They flowed here- and- there, but for the most part, it was hours of trying to get their sound— what they could do—perfect. The worship leader began to humiliate, embarrass, and publicly correct— not in love—these adult worship leaders, that were regional worship leaders already leading their own teams. It was obvious that this leader's focus was on what we could do and not what God could do in and through us as a team. So I left the second rehearsal feeling very inferior and down and discouraged.

I had decided that I was just going to pull out of the ministering for this event. But before I did that, I inquired of the Lord, and I knelt down at the side of the couch in my office, and I said, "Jesus, I know nothing, Please fill me with your everything and I'll take the next step forward into my destiny". Then suddenly I saw a snapshot of myself there with this team rehearsing, and the disgruntled look on that worship leader's face, and then God gave me this verse: Isaiah 43:25 says, "I, even, I am he who blots out your transgressions, for my own sake, and remembers your sins no more." Then I felt led to Hebrews 8:12, "For I will forgive their wickedness and will remember their sins no more." So, I said, God, I don't understand. I am not sinning by just deciding to not be a part of this group. And then, I read those two scriptures again, and I started to get the revelation of why God answered me with these two verses. The focus of these verses were not the sin or transgressions—the focus was on the fact that they both talk about God choosing "not to remember" something that we had done against him, because we repented of it.

So, then I realized that God has memory, because we know he is omniscient—"all knowing" about everything and everybody all the time. God was speaking to me, spirit to spirit, and he said, "Do you know why I love to hear you worship me and why it is so important to me?" And I said, "Lord, honestly, I know it's not the mediocre, less-than-perfect harmony part being sung, or my very basic level keyboard playing. Lord, I know what I get out of it, but what is in it for you? I really want to know. Can you tell me? I'm listening."

Then the Lord said, "I am your father, and you are my child, and when you worship me, you make memories with me, just like you would with an earthly father. I cherish these memories with my sons and daughters. Kelly, my memory is long, when it comes to you." Well, if that is all God said at that moment, it would have been enough, but he didn't stop there.

The Lord began to speak to me with snapshots of my life, as if I was his daughter and he was sitting next to me on my couch at home, and we had a photo album of my life opened. Only it was a living photo album—like power points out of a DVD that he had recorded and edited and gave narration to. (Even as I am writing this, my iphone is sitting next to me and just popped up a notification from Instagram from my son Gabriel. He is sending me his post of his wife, my daughter—I don't call her my daughter –in-law—that is too letter- of- the- law- that kills!! No, I call her my daughter, Jess. And she calls me Mom. Anyway, he just sent me a photo of Jess and my first granddaughter, Francesca, and a caption talking about her selflessness to take care of the needs of the family while he is on the ship in the Coast Guard. What was he doing by sending me this? He was making a memory with me—he was getting me to focus on a heartfelt emotion while he was being thankful for his wife—a blessing in his life.) This is a picture in the natural of what God was showing me happens in the spirit when we worship him-an eternal memory of the heart is shared. So while we are celebrating his goodness and mercy in worship, he is celebrating his love for us by creating an eternal memory in worship. That's what it means by heaven touching earth.

So while I am in this moment, watching this Imax screen with God, he begins to show me snapshots of my life. Then the Lord says, "I remember how you were living in that war zone with your parents, drinking themselves to death and practically killing each other. I remember how you would be up in your room with your guitar in hand, your little chord book, teaching yourself 3 chords so you could play one worship song off of the radio for me. I remember how you learned those 3 chords, and would worship me for hours, playing the same song, over and over again, and how you would sense my presence—and know my peace—even in the midst of the fear that you felt in your home, with guns going off and police busting down the door to remove your earthly father. I remember how, the worse things were in your house, you would worship me even more because of your desperate need for peace." Then I told the Lord, yes, I remember that, and I remember how, just when I thought my mother or us kids would be killed,, and it was the end for us, all of a sudden, God, you would intervene at the last moment, and save us all from that tragedy. Then, I would just worship you even more, Lord.

Then God showed me the next snapshot of me singing in a funeral parlor for my earthly father's funeral. My earthly father accepted Jesus as his Savior 3 years before he died, and we began to communicate again. God is so faithful!!! Well, at his funeral, I remember how I sang, "There Is Strength in the Name of the Lord". The anointing fell, and his wife that was his wife then, and all of my half brothers and sisters, that I had never met, stayed in touch with me after the funeral, and asked me for recording of my songs. I mailed them one cassette tape with a very elementary recording of my singing that song and a couple of worship songs with my guitar, and we corresponded for a while, and ultimately, they all accepted Christ into their hearts as Savior. Praise God! The Lord reminded me, that because I didn't hold a grudge against my earthly dad for all the beatings I received from him growing up, that because I went to that funeral parlor to bless my heavenly father—that God was able to use it for good and show his glory by saving my earthly father's family.

The next memory the Lord reminded me of was when I had just gotten divorced and I was working for a cleaning service, scrubbing other people's toilets and how I would strap a Walkman to my head and worship while I was cleaning these houses. While I cleaned for 14 hours a day, the presence of God would just show up and give me joy and take away all my fear. I knew that God had a plan for my life, and if I could just stay close to him, I would know it. During this period of time, so many people, who were Christians, were saying, "Do you know that your life is doomed now, because you got a divorce? Even if the man was abusive to you, don't you know that you and your children will never live out your destiny now"? I remember how I was crushed over hearing this from well- meaning Christians that judged me and then abandoned me. So I knelt down at my bed, and said, "God, is it true?" At that time, I knew divorce was a sin. I knew that there were consequences to it. But my question to God in that moment, was, "Am I on the damaged good pile? Will you ever use my ministry gifts again for you your glory"? You see, I repented from that sin, as soon as I did it. There was no reconciling with my soon to be ex-husband, because it was a done deal. So, when I repented, I asked God to forgive my sin, and for his mercy to follow my life in spite of my sin of divorcing an abusive man. (This is not an excuse for counseling people to divorce—I don't do that—this is my testimony of how God had me process it). As I asked the Lord this question, he said, "What sin didn't Jesus die for"? Then I thought about it, and I realized that he died for murder, lies, gossip, all the other sins listed in the Bible, but not divorce? He either died for ALL OR HE DIED FOR NONE. So, when these well-meaning people would come up and question me again, I would just ask them—"what sin didn't Jesus die for? He died for all, or he died for none. So I guess you have to decide for yourself. When you question the finality of the cross, you don't put me on trial, you put the blood of Jesus on trial."!! These people had no response to this—they would be silent and walk away. Am I saying that we can just sin that God's grace can keep on working? No, even the Bible says, in Romans 6:1 & 2: "Should we continue to sin that grace may abound? Certainly not!" Why is all this important? Because we need to understand that when we sin and repent, repent means that we turn around and do it God's way. However, we need to realize that God is not up on his throne with a bebe gun waiting for us to mess up, so that he can shoot us. He wants a relationship with us based on trusting that He knows best for us.

The next worship memory that me and Daddy God looked at together was a couple of days after my brother Michael had passed away. After God didn't resurrect him, after I prayed for God to, my brother had requested before he passed that I sing, "I Will Rise" for his funeral and bring my worship team in and do a worship service so many are saved and delivered. He wanted his passing to bring many sons and daughters to glory. So, as I was in my front room trying to get myself together to sing this, I just couldn't do it. I was mad at my brother for leaving and I was mad at God for letting him leave the earth. I recalled how, the night he passed, right before he passes away, I was in the hospital yelling at God at the top of my lungs to heal him—and crying and carrying on...and then God answered me and said, "I am not a will violator, why are you, Kelly?" And in that moment, I realized, that my brother was tired of his cancer battle and it was his wish to go to be with the Lord. So God gave me an instruction to go into my brother's room and whisper, "There is nothing else to do here. It's okay, go to Jesus." Then shortly later on that night, he was in glory with Jesus.

Well, as I was trying to prepare this song for his funeral, I kept weeping and couldn't complete it. All of a sudden, I saw a snapshot of my brother's face in front of me, and I sensed him saying, "It's okay, Kelly, Go to Jesus." So, I knelt down and named and sent every single emotion I was feeling to the feet of Jesus. As I did this, I felt God's presence fill up the room, and his peace rested on me, and I was able to sing and worship him again. Well, at the funeral parlor, both days, we had worship services and there was mass deliverance, and many souls came to accept Jesus as their Lord. There was such a glory cloud over those services that the funeral home director asked me for a business card to see if me and the worship team were available to do these services for other clients that would be holding services for their loved ones. The funeral home director and his wife were at the doorway weeping in the presence of God, and were changed. You cannot be in God's presence and not be changed.

These are just a few of the memories that the Lord gave me to show me that these are memories that he has recorded in heaven, but more than that, in his heart. He showed me other times where I was heartbroken or devastated or abandoned by those that were supposed to love and protect me, or rejected by my own, over and over again. He showed me how, the thing that impressed him to the point of saving that memory with me,, was that these memories remind Him, the Lord, of some of the most beautiful memories, because He, and I, together, made these times when my choice to worship, my song, sung out of the core of my being, in the darkest of times, was lifted up to Him and connected with Him spirit-to-spirit, and how he longs to make more of those memories with me. That's why I worship.

That's why I am here, because, for his good pleasure, all things were created, and my Daddy God takes pleasure in the memories that He and I have made together. I, his daughter, willingly chose Him, when I could have turned away from him, and blamed him!!! Wow!! Good times!!!!!

The best memories with Daddy God are made when we choose Him over our blinding pain, Him, over our hurt, Him, over worshipping the enemy by repeating his lies and his schemes.

So on the basis of that revelation, I made a decision to never question my own worship ability again. I decided that I will not worship the worship I can do, by man's standards, but that I will worship the King and make memories with a very loving Daddy God that is waiting there to make those memories and cherish them for eternity. There are those of you who are reading this book, and the world, your own flesh, and the devil has convinced you that the glory of God has departed off of your worship and that because of your past, even though you have repented of that, and are doing it God's way now, that your worship doesn't count!! Maybe another worship leader or pastor disqualified your gifts and talents or maybe you were fired from a worship team because you did not measure up! I am here to tell you that whatever was said, is a lie, and that you need to break off the Ichabod Curse that says there is no glory on your worship. I have been in your shoes; and even still, God has, and still creates so many opportunities for me to worship with other worshippers because I believe that He just wants to reminisce with me and have more memories to share with me. So that begs the question: Who or what has disqualified you from worshipping God, either corporately, in a service, or alone? God wants all of these moments with you to make memories.

If this is bearing witness with you, and you would like to break off the curse of Ichabod that is on your own personal worship, then do the next four steps:

1) Pray the "Prayer of Renunciation of the Ichabod Curse On My Worship" aloud.
2) Speak the "Decree a Thing" decrees aloud for the next 30 days.
3) Read the Prophetic Word concerning your worship out loud.
4) Complete the Prophetic Activation and write it down in a journal.

'PRAYER OF RENUNCIATION OF THE ICHABOD CURSE ON MY WORSHIP"

Heavenly Father, in the Name of Jesus, I identificationally repent on behalf of myself and my generational line, for all those, who spoke word curses over my worship, singing ability, musical ability, dance, or worship arts ministry skills and my expression of worship before you.

I renounce the word curses that indicated that the glory of God has departed off of my worship. Where

I have come into agreement with these lies in my heart, forgive me, Lord. I realize that you want me to worship you, not out of obligation, but because it pleases your heart to connect and make these memories with me.

Forgive me for all the times that I turned away from you in my darkest moments, because I was mad at you for that situation. Forgive me for trying to settle for a counterfeit form of false security to comfort me in hard times, instead of allowing your Holy Spirit to comfort me.

Forgive me Lord, for turning my face away from you, because I believed that my sins were too terrible, and that you, Lord, would not forgive them. I now know and believe and trust that when Jesus died on the cross, he nailed all my sins to the cross, and his sacrifice was enough. Forgive me for trying to do something to pay for my own sins, apart from his shed blood.

Father, forgive me, as a worship leader, or worship pastor, if I have, because of my own insecurity, bumped other people out of their spheres of authority in worship. Forgive me, Lord, for any negative, discouraging words I have spoken over your sons and daughters. Help me to speak life and encourage the gifts and be a good steward of the authority you have given me in this arena.

Father, you are my Daddy, God, and I am your child. I want to make memories with you in worship, both alone, and corporately, with the body of Christ. Make me willing to be willing to worship you, even when the storms of life come and try to knock me out of trusting you. Father, give me new songs in the night to praise you with. Activate my faith again, in the talents and gifts you have given me to worship you with.

I now, break, shatter, disintegrate, and destroy, all lies that have empowered the Curse of Ichabod to hinder my worship to your Lord. I break agreement with demons and all unholy alliances that have empowered these lies. I now send all fear, anxiety, shame, doubt, doublemindedness and unbelief to the feet of Jesus, to be used as a footstool. And in exchange, I receive the unconditional blessing of my Daddy God, and a new anointing from the Holy Spirit to worship my God with reckless abandonment, now and in the days to come.

Thank you, Father, for loving me enough to want to make memories of worship with me. Amen.

DECREE A THING

(Close your eyes and ask you spirit to turn around and connect with your Heavenly Father, then say the decrees out loud.)

- I decree that I will acknowledge you, Lord, in all of your ways.
- I decree that you, Lord, are restoring me with wisdom of the fear of the Lord.
- I decree that you, Lord, cleanse my senses from all defilement and enhance them for the glory of God.
- I decree that I will glorify Your name by finishing the work You, Lord, gave me to do.
- I decree that I will be patient, making allowances for my own and other's faults.
- I decree that the work Christ has begun in me will be completed.
- I decree that I will yield my will to the will of God.
- I decree that I will intentionally guard against division.
- I decree that you, Lord, are a very safe Daddy and that you wait, With joy, to spend time with me and make worship memories.
- I decree that I will live a life worthy of the calling I have received.
- I decree that I will always be humble and gentle.

THE PROPHETIC WORD

"FOR I SENSE THE LORD SAYING, "THE STRENGTH OF YOUR STORM IS NO MATCH FOR THE STRENGTH OF YOUR GOD, AND MY GREAT LOVE FOR YOU. MY STUBBORN LOVE WILL NOT LET GO OF YOU. I NEVER SLEEP, I NEVER SLUMBER, I AM THE GOD THAT WILL KEEP YOU FROM FALLING. I HOLD YOU IN THE GRIP OF MY GRACE AND A LOVE THAT WILL SUSTAIN YOU. DO NOT KEEP LOOKING AT THE STRENGTH OF YOUR STROM. DO NOT KEEP SPEAKING OF THE STRENGTH OF YOUR STORM. DO NOT KEEP PRAYING THE STRENGTH OF YOUR STORM. BUT LOOK UP, LOOK UP, LOOK UP, AND FOCUS ON THE STRENGTH OF YOUR GOD. SPEAK ABOUT MY STRENGTH, PRAY MY GREAT STRENGTH, DECREE MY STRENGTH OVER YOUR STORM, AND YOU WILL KNOW THAT I AM HOLDING YOU TIGHTLY IN THE MIDST OF YOUR STORM AND I WILL NOT LET YOU GO. YOUR STORM IS NO MATCH FOR OUR GOD, SAYS THE LORD. STOP WORSHIPPING YOUR STORM, AND WORSHIP MY GREAT NAME, SAYS THE LORD. THEN YOU WILL ARISE OUT OF YOUR HOPELESS PLACE AND THOSE AROUND YOU WILL SEE THAT I AM GREAT AND GREATLY TO BE PRAISED. I AM THE LORD AND THERE IS NO OTHER."

PROPHETIC ACTIVATION

1. Put soft worship music on and just thank God for three things that you are thankful for.

2. Ask Holy Spirit to reveal what some of your best memories that Daddy God has with you, when you worshipped him, or when you trusted him, when you so easily could have turned away.

3. Write down a couple of lines that express these memories, and how you know that God helped you overcome through worship to him.

CHAPTER FIVE

DETOXING FROM AN ICHABOD BELIEF SYSTEM AND GETTING DELIVERED FROM POVERTY MOUTH

"For as a man thinketh in his heart, so is he."
  -Proverbs 23:7

"Death and life are in the power of the tongue,
And those who love it will eat its fruit."
  -Proverbs 18:21

The case study is that of a woman, we will call her Janet, who came in to see me and told me she had a generational curse of misogyny (the hatred of women), and generational misandry (the hatred of men) in her family line. So in that session, we did a lot of work breaking that stuff off of her and her line through generational repentance prayers and a lot of other deliverance was done to cast things out that came in through these practices.

In the following session with Janet, she came in, and right at the beginning of the session, she began to give me the laundry list of confessions about how terrible her husband is. As she was speaking, she told me that she believed that he didn't even deserve her prayers and doesn't deserve God's mercy because of his secret addiction. Before even opening in prayer over the session, which I normally do at the beginning, the prophetic voice of God dropped on me and I began to release a word over her about her words. The prophetic word was:

"Why are you loosing the plan of the enemy over your Husband? When you do that, you are in total agreement with Satan who sits day and night telling the Father and Jesus accusations of why I shouldn't bless your husband. Now, will you agree with the enemy of your soul and put me in the position to withhold my blessing and deliverance?

Don't you know that when you speak, you are binding my good plan for you and your husband, in your house and in Heaven? Choose this day, whom you will serve, life or death, blessing or cursing, says the Lord."

Immediately, after I released that word, the spirit of God hit her with the word of truth and we invited the Holy Spirit in. As we did, she renounced and repented of her releasing the demonic over her husband, through her words, and broke agreement with the enemy. Then she asked the Holy Spirit to come in the room and re-baptize her with tongues of fire. We also prayed that God would release assigned seraphim angels to light on fire all that needed to be purified in her. Then she released a word of faith over her husband and declared the good things that God had for him. Within the next three days, that man began to turn around and walk out the plan of God for his life.

We could have been rebuking the devil and spirits working in him to come out and doing battle first, and we would not have seen any difference because we had to take care of legal things first. After she repented of getting legal things in place through her repentance, breaking agreement with the demonic, sending those spirits to the feet of Jesus for him to deal with, and then declaring openly the Word and the will of the Father for her husband, then she could cast out any residue demonic that was there. Then she continued to do spiritual warfare by holding her position of loosing the plan of God by her words, consistently making her confession line up with God's word and his will for her husband.

Every word we speak either binds the enemy's plans and looses God's plan or bind's God's plan and looses the enemy's plan. Your words are either doing one or the other. Start to ask yourself which are you doing, personally, in any given situation. Start to listen to those you work with; what are they doing with their confession and who are they giving power to? God or the enemy?

In Matthew 16, when Jesus came to the region of Casarea Phillippi, he asked his disciples, "Who do you say the Son of Man is"? They replied, "Some say that you are John the Baptist, others say Elijah, still others, Jeremiah or one of the prophets." The disciples words in these scriptures place them in agreement with the common view of Jesus, being that he was one of the great prophets come back to life, which many believe stems from Deuteronomy 18:18, where God said he would raise up a prophet from among the people.

Then, in Matthew 16:15, Jesus asks Peter, "But what about you?" Who do you say I am?" Then Peter replies, "You are the Christ, the Son of the Living God." So here, Peter confesses Jesus as divine and as the promised long-awaited Messiah. Then Jesus says, "Blessed are you, Simon, Son of Jonah, for this was not revealed to you a man, but by my Father in Heaven. And I tell you that you are Peter, and upon this rock, I will build my church and the gates of hell will not prevail against it." When Peter tells Jesus his revelation about his true identity, Jesus releases Peter's true identity and role in Kingdom purposes. When we get in agreement with Heaven, and the Father, and his will, then we become a place and a people for God to build his Kingdom on—for ourselves and for others.

Then, in Matthew 16:19, Jesus tells Peter a Kingdom principle. He says, "I will give you keys of the Kingdom inn heaven; whatever you bind on earth will be bound in heaven, and whatever you loose on earth will be loosed in heaven." Here in these verses, Peter heard from Heaven and released the will of the Father for Jesus over Jesus.

When we are in agreement with God's will, and our confession lines up, the Lord determines that we are a buildable lot. We have a worthy foundation to build on-Jesus-the chief cornerstone. Also in verse 19, Jesus gives Peter keys to represent the authority to carry out Kingdom work...church discipline, legislation, administration, to bring people to the kingdom of heaven by presenting them with the message of salvation found in God's Word. In

Matthew 28:16-19, Jesus tells his disciples that all authority in heaven and earth has been give to me. Therefore, on that authority of who Jesus is, we can go and make disciples of all nations, baptizing them in the name of the Father and the Son and the Holy Spirit, and teach them to obey everything Jesus has commanded to us.

Jesus gave Peter the keys to bind and to loose—and he has also given us the same authority in His Name. Luke 10:19 says, Behold, I give you power to tread upon serpents and scorpions and over all the power of the enemy, and nothing shall by any means hurt you." How do we bind and loose? By the words that we speak. I will prove this to you, by this next story about Peter's words. In Matthew 16: 21, it says, "From that time on Jesus began to explain to his disciples that he must go to Jerusalem and suffer many things at the hands of the elders, chief priests and teachers of the law, and that he must be killed and on the third day be raised to life." Verse 22 says that, "Immediately, Peter took Jesus aside and began to rebuke him. 'Never, Lord", he said. This shall never happen to you"!!

What did Peter just do? He used his authority to bind the plan of the God for Jesus. How did he do this? By using his words to loose the demonic over Jesus with his words. So Peter Just rebuked Jesus about doing his destiny—the same Peter who was just given the keys to the Kingdom. See, when we speak, we set an atmosphere for the demonic or for the plan of God for ourself and for others that we counsel, our families, other leaders, the marketplace, etc. It is very interesting to see how Jesus responded to Peter's binding God's will over Jesus. In verse 23, Jesus turned and said to Peter, "Get thee behind me, Satan! You are a stumbling block to me; you do not have in mind the things of God, but the things of men." Notice that Jesus didn't rebuke Peter, but dealt with the enemy who was trying to deceive Peter and release the demonic atmosphere over Jesus' destiny through Peter's words.

So we see in both the case study of my client, Janet, and the case study of Peter, that when we use mouth control, and only loose the plan of God, making sure that we are speaking things that God can use, it slams the door in the devil's face, especially when it comes to murmuring, complaining, finding fault, and grumbling.

Words have power. Proverbs 18:21 says, "Life and death are in the power of the tongue, and they that love it must eat its fruit." You have heard the expression, "you are what you eat"? Well, this is true also: "you become what you say." So our words have creative or destructive power. The Ichabod curse comes through others not discerning the will of God for our lives, and speaking things that are contrary, but it also come through word curses, and a curse is an implication of evil. It could be as simple as wishing someone ill, or not succeed in an area. A word curse does not have to be as sophisticated as conjuring some omen or hex or incantation, but sometimes they are casual. For example, someone may say in jest, "you will never get married, you will be just like your dad." Some others are, "You will never finish high school, or you will never finish your destiny or your calling."

Many of you that are reading this right now have dealt with this, and you are wondering, "Why am I not succeeding? If I get to a point, and the negative cycle or pattern starts all over again, and I don't finish in an area. Did you know that God spoke over Joshua that he would have "good success", which tells me that there is such a thing as bad success.

Word curses can also happen when someone who is in a position of authority speaks a word over us and we receive it. I was a victim of this myself. There were those who spoke over me, in authority and I came into agreement with what they spoke. Because of their position, because I respected the authority that they held, it caused me to come into agreement. There is a law of agreement. In Matthew 18, it says, "where two or more of you agree as touching anything", so even if you agree concerning something negative, you are still in agreement and are giving your consent for that negative to be loosed over your life. Word curses produce fear. Fear is faith in reverse. It is the anticipation and agreement with evil. Faith is the agreement with God's Word which cause us to hope for the manifestation of what he promised us. Well, fear is the agreement with the devil's lies that causes us to anticipate or expect evil.

So you must understand that when it comes to this issue of curses, that many of us subconsciously agree with curses spoken over our lives. You have agreed that when your grandmother told you, "you would never be married", that was the truth. You internalized the curse and you gave it power to act in your life. And this could be the reason why you are 60 and still not married—cause someone in authority spoke over you. This is also true when it comes to other pastors and leaders. There may be pastor in your region or territory that are speaking things against you. We can even have word curses in prayer where we begin to pray and speak words over people that are outside the will, plan and purpose of and they have your agreement or begin to get the agreement of other individuals against you. Many people will have opinions about you, both for good or for evil, however, when their opinions turn into word curses and you come into agreement with them, or they turn into slander and gossip against your name, then the enemy's plan is being loosed over your life. It is time to break those word curses.

I have had to break word curses over pastors that have come in my counseling office and said that inn a meeting, a prophet told then that they had a particular illness and wasn't sick at the time.

However, they got sick and had been battling that illness until we broke it. They had been battling it for years because someone in spiritual authority spoke it and they believed it and came into agreement with it. That is a word curse. Some others are, "you're stupid", "You're dumb", "you should have never been born", "you were a mistake", "you were born the wrong sex", "you were an accident", etc.

Galatians 4:13 says, that Jesus became a curse for us—so Jesus has broken the legal jurisdiction of the curse over the life of the believer, but you and I have to apply the blessing.

Someone reading this book might have a weight problem because someone told you that you will always be overweight and big-boned because everyone in your family was and you have wrestled with that for years. Someone else might be struggling in your marriage because of idol words of well-meaning family members. People, in jest may have said, "I give you one year, and you will be divorced. Your marriage will not make it past one year." You kind of laughed with them when they said it. When others say word curses over us, and we are silent, our silence is our agreement. Then all of a sudden, you are at the one year mark, and the relationship starts to fall apart, and you are wondering why. Someone in authority might have told you that your ministry would never prosper because they had a seed of jealousy in their heart and they spoke curses over your ministry. It happens very often in the church. Some of you may be harboring witchcraft within your intercessory team in your ministry. These individuals could be praying opposite to the will of God.

Some of the most common word curses that I have heard coming from clients over the years are:

- I AM NOT SPECIAL
- I WILL ALWAYS HAVE THESE ALLERGIES
- EVERYONE ALWAYS REJECTS ME
- THESE CHILDREN ARE GOING TO DRIVE ME TO DRINK.
- THIS SITUATION IS REALLY KILLING ME.

- I CAN'T (MEANING UNDERSTAND, COMPLETE THIS TASK)
- IF HE OR SHE DOES THAT AGAIN, I WILL GO OUT OF MY MIND
- THESE BILLS ARE BURYING ME, I WILL NEVER GET AHEAD
- IF I STOP SMOKING, I'LL EAT MORE AND GAIN WEIGHT
- I'LL NEVER STOP SMOKING
- I'LL NEVER LOSE WEIGHT
- MY SPOUSE WILL NEVER CHANGE
- IF I EAT ONE CHIP, I HAVE TO EAT THE WHOLE BAG
- I AM OUT OF CONTROL WITH SUGAR
- MY PARENTS TOLD ME THAT I HAVE MY DAYS AND NIGHTS MIXED UP WHEN I WAS A BABY, AND I STILL DO—I DON'T SLEEP AT NIGHT.

- I DON'T HAVE TIME TO GO TO THE GYM BECAUSE OF MINISTRY
- I WILL ALWAYS BE LEFT OUT, I'M JUST USED TO IT
- LIFE IS HORRIBLE
- I CAN'T TRUST ANYONE
- THAT'S JUST THE WAY THINGS ARE
- THAT'S JUST THE WAY I AM
- MY SIN IS UNFORGIVABLE
- I WILL ALWAYS BE LONELY
- I WILL ALWAYS BE SINGLE

This list could have been much longer, but I included it so that you can do some self-diagnosis to see if you have come into agreement with any of these word curses that are opposite of what the Word of God says you are, you can do, and what you have in Christ.

So what is the remedy? After we have concluded that we have come in agreement with these things, how do we come out of agreement with them and break the Curse of Ichabod off of our lives? I am glad you asked.

The following is a "Prayer Model for Disintegrating Word Curses".

PRAYER STEPS:

STEP I – Pray, "Heavenly Father, I invite you, Jesus and the Holy Spirit, here right now. Father, release security, protection, and identity over me right now. Jesus, release the revelation and truth of your promises to me and Holy Spirit, come and lead me and guide me into all truth concerning everything you want me to process right now. Holy Spirit, bring up a word curse that has been spoken over me, known, or unknown, so that I may extinguish the fiery darts of the enemy that are lodged inside of me. I do not want to live my life based on these word curses anymore."

STEP 2 – "Heavenly Father, I repent and renounce believing the word curse spoken to me that said: (take each one separately)"

_____

_____

Step 3 – "Lord, forgive me for believing these words, lies behind them, for living my life based on them, and for judging myself and others because of them."

Step 4 –" Lord, I forgive the person or persons who told them to me." (If you remember them by name, then name them) I forgive

_____

Step 5- " Lord, I break (clap one time while you say the word "break") agreement with demons and every unholy alliance that has held the power of this word curse/lie in place over me. I break, shatter, disintegrate, and destroy this word curse over my life. I send every lying spirit (name any other spirit you are discerning) back to the feet of Jesus now. "

Step 6: (place your hand over your heart):
" Lord, I replace this word curse with the truth of your Word that says," (look up a scripture verse that says the truth about you and write it in your journal or speak it out).

Step 7: " Lord, will you pour revelation of this Word deep into the place that was hurt and release a fresh anointing from your throne over me right now."

Step 8: " I decree that this word curse is broken over my life and I not long am required to think, act, speak, or operate based on it."

Step 9: Begin to memorize the scripture from Step 6 and recite it for 30 days aloud, into the atmosphere of your home.

WHY DO WE CLAP OUR HANDS AS WE ARE BREAKING AGREEMENT WITH THE NEGATIVE?

On many of these prayers for breaking our agreement with ungodly beliefs, when we come to the word, "break", we clap our hands while we say that word. Why do we do that? Well, for two reasons. The first is Biblical. The second reason is neurological.

The Biblical reason is found in three places in the Old Testament.

*Nahum 3:19 – refers to clapping ones hands over something wicked being destroyed.

"Nothing can heal your wound. Your injury is fatal. Everyone who hears the news about you claps his hands at your fall, for who has Not felt your endless cruelty?"

This scripture was spoken from Nahum over the city of Ninevah, where, generations after they had repented from Jonah's message, evil reigned again. So Nahum prophesied that the proud and powerful nation would be utterly destroyed because of its sins. (Trauma is endless to the one who has endured it and carried it for years)

*Job 27:23 – refers to clapping ones hands against the wicked one. V.13..."here is the fate God allots to the wicked. V.20....."terrors overtake him like a flood, V. 21-23, "the east wind claps its hand in derision, and hisses him out of his place."

These scriptures, in context, is Job talking about the fate of the wicked, But never agrees he is in this group of people, but he is righteous in God, no matter what!

*Lamentations 2:15 – refers to clapping ones hands in judgment over wrongdoing. .

"All who pass your way clap their hand at you. They scoff and shake their Heads at Daughter Jerusalem and say, "Is this the city that was called the Perfection of beauty, the joy of the whole earth?" Jeremiah wrote the book of Lamentations. This was written soon after the fall of Jerusalem in 586 B.C. The setting is that Jerusalem, has been destroyed by Babylon and her people killed, tortured, or taken captive. Jeremiah wept because the people rejected their God.

In Bible days, clapping was used in worship, but it was also used as a type of protest or rebuke against something. (Hebrew "machot" www.adath-shalom.ca/hebrew words history.htm

The second reason for the power of a clap in these deliverance prayer models is neurological. In short, the negative emotion stored in the Amygdala part of the brain, can be separated from the actual memory stored in the Hippocampus, or the memory storehouse of the brain, when prayer ministry is coupled with a loud noise, such as a clap. The loud clap opens up the Reticular Formation of the brain and the negative emotional triggers attached to a trauma event, or word curses, or an ungodly belief system, are diffused. What does that mean? It basically means that where your brain, neurologically has been empowering the liar, through believing the lies, which is how the demonic attaches to us, is basically disempowered, or dethroned off of our brains and neuro-transmitters. They are thrown right off of the neuro-highway. So even if a person has the memory of the hurt, they will have no hurt of the memory. A sharp clap, coupled with authoritative prayer to cancel and nullify the power of the lies or negative memory, followed by naming the negative emotions or behavior itself,,, then, while the reticular formation is still open, following up with the truth of scripture, and a blessing, will replace the negative memory or ungodly belief. That is why I have you doing prayers, decrees, blessings and prophetic activations at the end of each chapter. You have spent too many years empowering the lies and the liar—Satan, now you can spend some time empowering the truth and the Truth Giver, Jesus Christ through the Holy Spirit. At first this method may seem strange, however, many deliverance ministers use this method, because it breaks triggers at a neurological level.

Too much information? Okay…… moving on.

****

We cannot address the power of our words without addressing the power of our belief systems. Why? In Luke 6: 45, it says, "the good person, out of the good treasure of his heart produces good things; and the evil person out of his evil treasure produces evil, for out of the abundance of the heart, his mouth speaks."

Some conflict is internal and some is external. But it is not what is happening around you that will bury you—it is what you believe about it. You cannot rise any higher than your own confession and your own confession comes out of your own belief system or pattern of beliefs. We have to train ourselves to have a godly pattern of beliefs before we can ever counsel others to do so. You're level of influence in those you minister to will only come up to your own confession and belief system. Our belief pattern will decide whether we give in or bend under the pressure.

The key is to speak the Word of God long enough to give God something to work with so that he can enforce His plan in the issue or people involved in the conflict.

What is a belief system? It is our beliefs, decisions, attitudes, agreements, judgments, expectation, vows and oaths. Any beliefs that agree with God, his Word, His nature, or His character constitute our godly beliefs. Any beliefs that do not agree with Go, His Word, His nature, or his character contribute to our ungodly beliefs. As the Holy Spirit cleans our minds, our belief system begins to change from a mixture of mostly ungodly beliefs to more and more godly beliefs. A godly belief is reflected in our actions and a godly belief is rooted in our heart. If you are not in God's Word, you will be influenced by the devil and his lies. When you believe the lies, you empower the liar. Christian people can be bothered and afflicted by the devil. You soul still needs to be renewed and your body can be influenced. What you believe becomes an action. An action becomes a habit. A habit becomes a stronghold. A stronghold becomes a destiny.

In Matthew 3: 16 &17, Jesus is being baptized in the Jordan River by John the Baptist, and God, the Father says to him, "this is my son, in whom I love and in whom I am well pleased." We have that wonderful scene in the bubble, when all of a sudden, a few verses later in Matthew 4: 1-3, Jesus is lead into the wilderness to be tested by God and tempted by the devil. Jesus is about to be promoted into his earthly ministry, and Father God wanted to see if Jesus' belief system and his confession would stand up to the temptation of the devil. Greater than that, Father God wanted to see if Jesus would give God final word over the temptations. Here Jesus models to us how to deal with the ungodly beliefs of the enemy. Jesus uses what I call, "the win then fight" strategy in order to defeat the enemy. Jesus won the battle in his own mind by fasting in order to beat his flesh down that wanted to rule. He placed his soul beneath his spirit so that his mind will and emotions would not be allowed to rule when the pressure was on.

When we are in this battle of being tempted by the devil, our mind says, "this isn't happening fast enough, I guess it never will. So we prophecy our outcome. When we are in this battle, our emotions say, "That doesn't feel good—being beaten down to be made subject to the Lord's timing and His way, so I will have to be my own boss and take charge." When this is happening, our will says, "I want to give up because it's too hard, I want what is familiar and comfortable, like an old blanket on a rainy day." Proximity to Jesus, staying close to Daddy God during the temptation to quit or take unrighteous control, is a key to overcoming. When we do this, we will allow our spirit part of us to rule, and be in the driver' seat, and then our soul will have to be buckled up in the passenger seat, ready to go anywhere our spirit man, guided by the Holy Spirit, wants us to go.

The first ungodly belief that Satan came after Jesus with, was one to cast doubt on his identity in his Father God. Father God had just told him that he is the Son of God, and Satan comes along and says, "If you are the Son of God, then, tell these stones to become bread." Satan's #1 goal of his ungodly beliefs is to get us to believe that we might not be who God says we are. In case you are wondering who you are to God, I am going to spell it out for you and make it plain. When he told Jesus who he was to him, he told us who we are because we are in Christ Jesus. First, we are God's chosen sons and daughters. Secondly, we are deeply loved by the Father, and thirdly, we are highly favored by God. Jesus passed the first test by saying, "Man does not live by bread alone, but by every word that comes out of the mouth of God." In other words, I am giving my father final word that what he says trumps what you say about me.

Satan met Jesus with the #2 ungodly belief that says, "In order to secure a position in God, Jesus would have to do something to prove that what His

Father said about His was absolutely true. In this passage, Satan tempts Jesus by saying, "If you are the son of God, then throw yourself down from this highest point of the temple." Jesus answered, "Do not put the Lord your God to the test." One of Satan's job is to destroy us before we ever begin our calling. Satan met Jesus with the #3 ungodly belief that says Jesus could fulfill his divine destiny without a cross. Satan led Jesus up to a very high mountain and told him that he could have all of it if Jesus would bow down and worship him. Jesus said, "Away from me, Satan. For it is written, 'Worship the Lord your God, and serve him only." We don't get to fulfill our divine destiny apart from the cross and being obedient to the process. Jesus was obedient to the process and we will also have to be.

So Jesus prepared his flesh by fasting, quickly responded to the enemy's lies, gave his Father, final word, by saying, "It is written", reminded himself and the enemy of his true identity by speaking out the godly belief and confessing the truth of God's Word. The only Word that will come out of us in a temptation is the Word that we put in us. We have to very quickly tell the enemy, "ACCESS DENIED."

Let's look at this example of Peter. I know, I am always picking on him, right? He is just such a good case study and one that so many of us can relate to. This story shows us so many ungodly beliefs that have to be replaced with the truth. This story comes from Luke 5:1-11. Simon Peter as washing his nets and he was finished so he was letting Jesus use his boat to preach to the people. When we let God use what little we have, he brings the increase and gives us more of what He has—his resources, his strength, his money, etc. So Jesus told Simon Peter, who had already washed his nets, and thought his days was over, to let down his net for a catch. It took faith for Peter to do this, to go back out again. It takes faith, after failure, to try again, because just when you have decided in your own mind, that you have gone as far as you are going to go, and maybe it's not meant for me to catch anything, get married, move up any higher in my job, move up any higher in my calling, have children, start a new business, etc., God says, "let down your net". Some of you are frustrated right now because you are still washing your nets, as if it's over, when God is saying, "Try again."

Simon, speaking back to Jesus, says, "We have toiled all night and caught nothing, but nevertheless, at your word, I will let down the net. Next, it says, that "When they had done this they caught a great multitude of fish. Can you believe that God has something great for you at a time that you were washing your nets? It is amazing how you can go from failure into a massive release of blessings so quickly. The Bible says, "and the nets had to break", so they beckoned to their partners" to help with the overage of fish. When God blesses, you should always take someone with your, cause we can do more together than we can alone. Even the partners couldn't stand the blessing and release coming on them. The Bible says that they went from failing and sinking to such a blessing of a release, that even their partners' boats began to sink from the weight of the haul of fish.

Some of you reading this book have lost your houses, cars, jobs, and are living with parents or children or family and you are living with the bare minimum to get by. There are some keys here that we all need to heed to get us back in the game that have do with our confession and our belief system. This is one of the most consistent messages that we have to keep going back to in order to keep winning the battle in our own minds and help others to win theirs.

The main idea about what Peter believed in this whole story, or the take away from this lesson is that when Simon Peter saw the blessing of the next phase or level that God was pouring over his life, instead of dancing and shouting and having a moment of spiritual glory expressed, the Bible says in verse 8 that he fell down at Jesus's knees saying, "Depart from me; for I am a sinful man, Oh, Lord." Isn't that a weird reaction to a blessing? He is now taking the lead and instead of him taking the lead, he is now rejecting the opportunity.

Why? Because sometimes life will offer you a blessing, but because you still perceive yourself as being in the back, you are not ready to receive the blessing on this next level of life, not because of external conflict, cause now, everything externally is going well. Just because something is going well externally, doesn't mean that things are going well internally, or inside of us.

You're gift can take you some places that your mind isn't ready for or your character isn't ready for; your self-perception isn't ready for and you will reject the blessings and say, "Just leave me alone, leave me back here washing my nets because you have gone and done it—you have scared me."

In the next verse, Jesus says to Peter, "Fear not, for from this moment forward, you will catch men." When they had brought their ships to land, they forsook all and followed Him and the whole issue here was fear of the next level, taking the next step, fear of the unknown and going forward. Much of our internal conflict and those we minister to and counsel, is because of our or their belief systems.

We are going to look at some common beliefs that keep us beneath what Christ died to give us. As long as you believe these lies, you are under their influence and your belief requires you to think, act, choose, judge others and judge yourself by them.

"I am afraid to fail." This is a belief system rooted and grounded in a Fear of failure. Some of the confessions that come out of this belief are, or "I'm not going to own anything, cause I might lose it.", or "I'm not going to buy a house, cause I might lose it, or I'm not going to get married because I might get divorced." Have you ever given yourself permission to succeed? Or are you so intimidated by the fear of failure that you don't try? The belief in this, at the core level is, **"I will erect a wall of hopelessness that will keep me from hoping so that I will never be disappointed."** The only problem with that thinking is that "faith is the substance of things hoped for—the evidence of things not seen. God rewards our faith, and he is pleased when we trust him with things that seem too big for us. So if we can do it without God, he probably isn't in it. The opposite of faith is not doubt or fear, it is sight. 2 Corinthians 5:7 says, "we walk by faith, not by sight." If you can provide it and see it, and measure it, than God probably isn't in it.

Another common ungodly belief is, **"I am afraid of success."** This is the belief that you will reach your goal, but some disaster may result. **The mindset is, "I want it, but I don't want all the stuff, or pressure that comes with it."** When you reject God's opportunity, you are left with the consequences of your own confession and you believe that some way, you will get the blessing up at the top, while you are staying in the low place. It is like believing God that you are going to get pregnant and not gain weight, or saying, "I want the baby, but I don't want the stretch marks, or morning sickness." All of that is part of the process. If you allow anyone or anything to talk you out of a moment of opportunity, then you will forfeit it. You will be stuck washing your nets when there is a great multitude of fish waiting for you if you had the courage to believe. What really stops an individual from taking the next step is not the lack of talent, resources, or education. You can be highly educated and failing and homeless. Education alone is not the solution. People can be educated and stuck. We can become educated beyond our faith, so that we don't need out faith anymore. Very gifted people are homeless and incarcerated. Ask yourself right now, "What am I doing to sabotage my own success of moving to the next level?" As others are elevated, you can become jealous or bitter or you can challenge yourself to say, "What is wrong with my belief systems that are stopping me from going to the next level in this area?"

This is not just about money or prestige, it is about profess. It is not God;s will for us to live, live long and have no progress. When I counsel individuals, I give them homework as obtainable growth goals to get them in a pattern of seeing and believing that lines up with the confession for God and His beliefs about them. God's will is that we progress in parenting, marriage, work, ,and making our worship a heart of gratitude toward him a lifestyle. It takes a lot of energy and a great commitment to hold onto and manifest a bitter root. But we will talk about dealing with bitter roots in another chapter.

The next ungodly belief I want to look at is, **"I do not deserve the good measure of success."** This flows out of a shame-based belief system, which is fueled by a poverty spirit, the Curse of Ichabod's fruit in an orphaned heart. Shame does not say that "I made a mistake, and if I repent, God will forgive me, and then I can just keep on going." No, shame says, "I am a mistake", and so the cardinal rule of shame is that "I must hide", because if anyone really finds out who I am or what I have done, they will reject me." Shame tries to keep the true self hidden from God and others. The poverty spirit keeps you in a place of believing that there will never be enough of anything. There will never be enough money for you, time for you, good health for you, or the time, attention, or affection of God or other people in your life. It keeps you constantly distrustful of God's abundance and a need to hold onto everything you have tightly because if you don't there is no more coming. This belief is opposite of the Kingdom mindset. The Bibles says, "Give and it will be given unto you, pressed down, shaken together, and running over."

We see one of the results of The Curse of Ichabod being this poverty mentality. We see this with the story of the prodigal sons. The story of the prodigal sons in Luke 15:11-32, is the story of two sons with an orphan spirit. The younger son spends his inheritance in pursuit of pleasure. Pain always pursues pleasure. The older son works to earn his father's love and not realizing he already has his father's favor. The orphan/poverty spirit manifests in one of two ways in a life: either the person goes to rebellion, seeking pleasure, addiction, compulsion, lust of the flesh, lust of the eyes, and will try to medicate the pain of being abandoned and the belief that they are fatherless, like the younger son did. He rebelled. The second way an orphan spirit manifests is through religion—working and striving to get in to performance orientation so that God and the people around them will accept and love them. The older son fell into this religious cycle and the older son represents many in the church who believe they are close to God, but in reality, don't know God. Both sons lived as orphans with a poverty spirit. They both lived in constant fear of lack and a negative heart expectancy—always expecting the worst and the least for themselves. The younger son asked for his inheritance early and tried to spend it right away because he was afraid it would be gone if he waited for the father to pass. The older son stayed homme to try to earn favor with his father because he lived in constant fear of lack of love and acceptance from his father.

There are also cultural beliefs that oppose God's truth that we need to deal with. Probably every people group has characteristics that become strongholds or patterns of thinking within their own culture. Paul Cox, a deliverance mentor of mine, gives evidence of this, in his book, *"Come Up Higher"*, when he mentions a testimony from Cindy Jacobs, of Generals of Intercession. While she was visiting Norway, an intercessor named Laura, who had been praying in Norway, came to her. She handed Cindy a list of "laws" that most Scandinavians are aware of, cultural assumptions that govern their society This woman Laura, told Cindy Jacobs, that this list represented one of the major strongholds that hinder many Scandinavians from coming into their fullness as believers. The list is as follows:

1. You shall not think that you are special.
2. You shall not think that you have a good standing.
3. You shall not think that you are smart.
4. Don't fancy yourself as being better than anyone else.
5. You shall not think that you know more than anyone else.

6. You shall not think that you are more important than anyone else.
7. You shall not think that you are good at anything.
8. You shall not laugh.
9. You shall not think that anyone cares about you.
10. You shall not think that you can be taught.

This list was called the Jante Laws. They not only affected those of Scandinavia, but also places where the people of Scandinavia have settled as well. These laws can have many effects. They would put a lid on worship when shouting louder than others is see as speaking up too much in public. Also, they would stop the giving of "honor to who honor is due", because that would be acting as if someone were more important than another. The apostles and five-fold ministry could not rise up because they might fancy themselves to be better than others. People from almost every culture may be victims of unexamined cultural beliefs, patterns, and traits that perpetuate iniquities and cause them to continue to be passed down the family line and keep the Curse of Ichabod alive and well in the bloodline. I have seen these Jante Laws also show up in the counseling room often, coming out of the mouths of the clients, as their own personal belief systems. These beliefs go against everything God has said about us in his Word, and they reinforce the lie that "the glory of God has departed from us" and that "the glory of God was never on us, to begin with."

If you see yourself in this section of this chapter, and realize that you have many ungodly beliefs that have been holding you back from going forward to be all that you were created to be, then do the following steps to break free of these lies:

1. Pray the "Prayer to Break Free of Conformity" (Jante Stronghold) aloud.
2. Read the Prophetic Word aloud.
3. Say the decrees in "Decree a Thing" aloud for the next 30 days.
4. Diagnose your own ungodly beliefs and use the "Replacing Ungodly Beliefs with Godly Beliefs" prayer tool on a regular basis.
5. Once you begin your godly belief journal, write the godly beliefs or the truth, and then the scripture that reinforces the godly belief. Read these every day, so that when the devil comes to try to whisper the old lie to you, you can speak the new godly belief and send the enemy packing!!! You can even begin your new godly belief journal using the scriptures listed in the prayer below, and look them up and write them out. Memorize them and say them every time you begin to doubt the truth.

PRAYER TO BREAK THE SPIRIT OF CONFORMITY (JANTE STRONGHOLD)

1. I break (clap) the mindset that I am not special. The truth is I am awesome because I am created in His, God's image. (I Peter 2:9)
2. I break (clap) the mindset that I am not important. The truth is I am Important to God (Ephesians 2:14-18; I Corinthians 12:12)
3. I break (clap) the mindset that others are wiser than me. The truth is I have the Holy Spirit living inside of me and He gives me supernatural wisdom. (James 1:5)
4. I break (clap) the mindset that others are better than me. The truth is God has given me purpose and destiny to be a success. (Jeremiah 29:11)
5. I break (clap) the mindset that others are more important than I am.
   The truth is that I am precious and honored in His sight. (Isaiah 43:4, John 3:16)
6. I break (clap) the mindset that others know more than I do. The truth is I know God who knows all. (I Corinthians 3:16, Romans 8:11)
7. I break (clap) the mindset that I am not good at anything. The truth is God has given me unique talents and gifts to benefit others. (I Corinthians 12:7-11)
8. I break (clap) the mindset that no one can laugh at me. The truth is that God is joyful over me. (Luke 5:11-32)

9. I break the mindset that no one cares about me. The truth is God loves me. (I Peter 5:7, Romans 12:10)
10. I break (clap) the mindset that no one can teach me anything. The truth is I am a disciple who is constantly learning from God and others. (Matthew 28:19-20.

(NOTE: IF YOU ARE UNCOMFORTABLE WITH CLAPPING WHEN YOU SAY THE WORD, "break", THEN JUST DO THE PRAYER WITHOUT ADDING THE CLAPS WHERE THEY ARE PLACED.)

PROPHETIC WORD

"FOR THE LORD SAYS UNTO YOU, 'WILL YOU REBUKE YOUR GIANTS OR LAY DOWN IN FRONT OF THEM? WILL YOU SPEAK TO YOUR MOUNTAIN OR LET IT CRUSH YOU? I SAY YOU HAVE THE POWER TO CURSE THE MOUNTAINS AND THE GIANTS THAT STAND IN YOUR WAY BLOCKING ALL THE PROMISES. HAVE NOT TOLD YOU, "BEHOLD, I GIVE YOU POWER TO TREAD UPON SERPENTS AND SCORPIONS AND OVER ALL THE POWER OF THE ENEMY, AND NOTHING SHALL BY ANY MEANS HARM YOU." 'WILL YOU BE POWERFUL OR POWERLESS IN THIS SEASON OF YOUR LIFE? I SAY, TAKE OUT THE TRASH, TODAY. TAKE THE WRECKLESS WORDS, THE SHARDS OF GLASS THAT OTHERS HAVE THROWN AT YOU TO CUT YOU, AND DEMOLISH THEM. I SAY, REJECT THE WORDS THA CAME FROM OTHERS WHEN THEY TRIED TO DUMP THEIR TOXIC WAST INTO YOUR LIFE, WITH THEIR WORDS. I SAY, TAKE THE TRASH

OUTSIDE OF YOUR BODY, MIND, AND EMOTIONS BY REJECTING EVERYTHING THAT GOES AGAINST WHAT I HAVE TOLD YOU THAT YOU ARE, YOU HAVE, AND CAN DO. NO LONGER LAY DOWN IIN FROONT OF YOUR GIANT AND LET HIM OVERTAKE YOU. I SAY, ARISE AND OPEN YOUR MOUTH AND MY LGORY WILL SHINE ON YOU AND MY WORD IN YOUR MOUTH WILL SEND YOUR GIANT FLEEING 7 DIFFERENT WAYS. SPEAK TO YOUR GIANT. DEMAND RETRIBUTION OF ALL THAT'S BEEN LOST. TAKE BACK YOUR DIGNITY, YOUR HONOR AND THE JOY WE HAVE TOGETHER, THAT IS YOUR STRENGTH. YOU ARE TOO HIGH TO LIVE THAT LOW. COME UP HERE, AGAIN, INTO THE HEAVENLY PLACES WITH ME."

DECREE A THING

- I DECREE THAT I HAVE THE MIND OF CHRIST RESIDING IN MY INNER MAN.
- THE MIND OF CHRIST LIVES BIG IN ME AND IS FULL OF ALL KNOWLEDGE, WISDOM, INSIGHTS, UNDERSTANDING, AND SOLUTIONS THAT I NEED.
- I POSSESS "DIVINE INTELLIGENCE".
- I DO NOT LEAN ON MY OWN UNDERSTANDING,, BUT IN ALL MY WAYS, I ACKNOWLEDGE GOD.
- GOD'S WAYS ARE HIGHER THAN MY WAYS; THEREFORE I HUMBLE MYSELF BEFORE HIM AND RECEIVE HIS UNDERSTANDING.

- **THROUGH THE MIND OF CHRIST, I CAN ACCESS THE KNOWLEDGE OF WITTY INVENTIONS.**
- **THE MIND OF CHRIST REVELAS THINGS I NEED TO KNOW ABOUT THE FUTURE.**
- **THE MIND OF CHRIST TEACHES ME TO MAKE GODLY DECISIONS DAILY.**
- **THE MIND OF CHRIST GRANTS ME MEMORY AND RECALL.**
- **I HAVE THE ABILITY TO RETAIN KNOWLEDGE.**

REPLACING UNGODLY BELIEFS WITH GODLY BELIEFS TOOL

BIBLICAL STRATEGY:

Romans 21:1 says, "Do not be conformed to the patterns of this world, But be transformed by the renewing of your mind. Then you can test what is good, acceptable, and The perfect will of God."

METHOD: to legally break our agreement with the ungodly belief and to legally join in agreement with God. Satan is a legalist and God will not forcefully break Any belief that we have made with the world, the flesh, or the devil—we have to make the choice to break it. Doing this makes all of the difference in the ease of acquiring a belief system in alignment with God's Word, nature, and character.

PROCEDURE:

1. IDENTIFY THE UNGODLY BELIEF OR THOUGHT. HOLY SPIRIT WILL EXPOSE THE FEARS, WORRIES, ANGER, HRUTS, BITTERNESS, OR BLAMING ROOT ATTACHED TO THIS AS YOU SPEAK IT OUT OR WRITE IT OUT.

2. WRITE OUT THE GODLY BELIEF—WHAT THE OPPOSITE OF THE LIE THAT YOU HAVE BEEN BELIEVING MAY BE. IF YOU DON'T KNOW, SAY, "HOLY SPIRIT, WHAT IS THE TRUTH ABOUT THE LIE I HAVE BEEN BELEIVING?" GODLY BELIEFS WILL NEVER CONTRADICT WHAT GOD HAS TOLD US IN HIS WORD. THEY WILL ALWAYS LINE-UP. ALWAYS.

3. USE SCRIPTURE TO VERIFY THE NEW GODLY BELIEF. WRITE OUT THE SCRIPTURE. WRITE OUT MORE THAN ONE AS HOLY SPIRIT GIVE THEM. IF YOU ARE NOT SURE, EITHER USE A CONCORDANCE, OR GO TO YOUR SMARTPHONE, AND GOOGLE BIBLE VERSES ABOUT GOD'S LOVE FOR ME, OR BIBLE VERSES ABOUT GOD'S PROMISES TO ME, ETC.

4. MINISTER TO THE BELIEF SYSTEM THROUGH PRAYING THIS MODEL PRAYER. (THIS IS THE KYLSTRA'S RTF MODEL)

   A. I CONFESS MY SIN AND MY ANCESTOR'S SIN OF BELIEVING THE LIE THAT

   _____

B. I FORGIVE THOSE WHO HAVE CONTRIBUTED TO MY FORMING THIS LIE. (BE SPECIFIC, NAME THEM)

C. I ASK YOU, LORD, TO FORGIVE ME FOR RECEIVING THIS LIE, FOR LIVING MY LIFE BASED ON IT, AND FOR ANY WAY THAT I HAVE JUDGED OTHERS BECAUSE OF IT. I RECEIVE YOUR FORGIVENESS.

D. ON THE BASIS OF YOUR FORGIVENESS, LORD, I CHOOSE TO FORGIVE MYSELF FOR BELIEVING THIS LIE.

E. I RENOUNCE AND BREAK MY AGREEMENT WITH THIS LIE. I CANCEL MY AGREEMENT WITH THE POWER OF DARKNESS. I BREAK ALL AGREEMENTS I HAVE MADE WITH DEMONS.

F. I CHOOSE TO ACCEPT, BELIEVE, AND RECEIVE THE GODLY BELIEF THAT

_____

(NAME THE TRUTH THAT IS THE OPPOSITE OF THE LIE)

G. PRAY, MEDITATE AND THINK ABOUT THE NEW GODLY BELIEF OR TRUTH FOR AT LEAST 30 DAYS, SO THEY ARE WELL ROOTED AND BEGIN TO MANIFEST AS EVERYDAY TRUTH IN YOUR LIFE.

H. WRITE THE NEW BELIEF IN YOUR JOURNAL AND BEGIN TO MAKE A LIST OF ALL YOUR NEW BELIEFS AND PRETTY SOON, YOUR NEW BELIEF SYSTEM WILL BE REPLACING THE OLD ONE.

CHAPTER SIX

THE BIRTHMARK OF A GLORY DWELLER

"Even though I walk through the valley of the shadow of death, I will fear no evil; for You are with me; Your rod and staff, they comfort me." - Psalm 23:4

"When you pass through the waters, you will not drown; when You pass through the fire, the flames will not consume you." - Isaiah 43:2

I believe that each and every one of us are in a "passing through" moment every day of our lives, and corporately as the body of Christ right now in this prophetic hour. Every day we wake up, we have to decide what kind of man or what kind of woman we are going to be. Are we going to storm the gates of hell with a glory storm by using the weapons of our warfare and kick the gates of hell in, or are we going to allow the gates of hell to storm our life and control our destiny?

The anointing of God is His Presence to allow us to do his will for our lives. God's glory is His Proximity to us, or I should say, our proximity to Him, that only come from spending time with him, so that we are transformed, as the Bible says, "from glory to glory" over time. What does that mean exactly? Well, our case study in this chapter is of Jesus, and of Moses. Moses is a type or a shadow, in the Old Testament, of type of Christ, because we know that Moses was a deliverer to the children of Israel, and Jesus also delivered humankind through the victory of the cross. God's glory is more than the weight of his power and his tangible presence. We get a key to dwelling in this glory, when, in Exodus 33:18, Moses asks the Lord to show him His Glory. Then in verse 19, The Lord says, "I will cause my goodness to pass in front of you, and I will proclaim my name, the Lord, in our presence. So the Lord, from the cloud, starts to proclaim his name, and says, "I am the Lord, slow to anger, abounding in lovingkindness, merciful, forgiving, and he starts to name all these attributes of his nature and his essence." So Moses tried to see the glory, and God gave him a glimpse into the depth and the nature of who God is.

So I believe that when we say we want to have the Lord's glory, or we want to be filled with the Lord's glory, it is more than just chill bumps on our arms and feeling the anointing, or being touched by the presence of God. There is a very deep realm of knowing who God is. Who did God have compassion on? Who did he have mercy on? On us, on all of humanity, by making a way—giving his only son Jesus, to die on a cross for us so we would not have to be in an eternal hell with Satan, after we leave this earth. He also did this because he wanted to have a relationship with us and wanted us to want a relationship with him. So we see here that the key to being a glory dweller is knowing the nature, the character of God and then allowing that nature to so touch us and so fill us that we begin to overflow in

God's presence, but also to walk in the very nature of God himself, in his kindness and longsuffering, and compassion on those who hurt us. This includes all of his conviction, as we are transformed into his image by his glory. Being transformed by the anointing so we can complete our assignment, yes, but literally coming in to the character of God by his glory, is the ultimate goal.

One of the characteristics of a glory dweller is one who is able to forgive an offense quickly. Based on the scripture in Exodus that we just read, God's glory is his goodness.

We cannot be in a service or a meeting where God's glory falls on us and then leave that meeting and go out and pick up holding a grudge against the person we were cursing about on the way to the meeting. In these scriptures in Exodus, it is evident that God's heart is to forgive, and contend with his people. Jesus inherited this nature from his Daddy God, because we see that he was willing to go to the cross and die for each one of us so that we could go free.

According to Matthew 6: 14-15, forgiveness is not an option. "For if you forgive men for their transgressions, your heavenly father will forgive you. But if you do not forgive men, then your Father will not forgive your transgressions." I John 1: 9 says, "If we confess our sins, He is faithful and just to forgive us and to cleanse us From all unrighteousness."

When Jesus was on the cross, he spoke 7 things at 7 different times. The very first thing he said was, "Forgive them, Father, for they don't know what they are doing." Jesus realized that everything that was happening to him was Father-filtered. Christ understood that the crucifixion was planned and that the Father had sent him to earth for this. Jesus forgave those who were offensive to him on every level. The biggest moment of Jesus' life is the cross and He stops dying to say, "Father, forgive them." Why? Because he wants to throw up every weight so he can get up in 3 days and be at maximum when he rises and secures and seals his destiny.

To the degree that any of us hold onto bitterness, we block God from doing the very thing that he intends to do through the pain for us and the Kingdom.

I have so many clients that come into my office and say, "I have forgiven them, but I have not forgotten". They use that statement to justify still holding bad feelings toward their offender. My response to that is always the same: "Of course you haven't forgotten, cause that is impossible. Forgiving is not forgetting.

Do you think that Jesus was in denial when he was on the cross and his blood was mangled with our pain and sin? No, he never denied his suffering, he made a choice when he said, "Forgive them, Father, for they don't know what they are doing." FORGIVENESS IS NOT FORGETTING, IT IS CHOOSING NOT TO REMEMBER!!! If God is all-knowing, which he is, then he can never erase his memory; but he casts our sins into the sea and chooses not to remember. This is how he doesn't hold our sins against us. Hebrews 8:12 reminds us, "For I will forgive their wickedness and will remember their sins no more." Micah 7:19 says, "You will again have compassion on us; you will tread our sins underfoot and hurl all our iniquities into the depths of the sea." God puts all of our sins in the depths of the sea, and he then puts up a "No Fishing" sign. "Hebrews 10:17, "Their sins and their lawless deeds I will remember no more." Revelation 12:10 says, "Then I heard a loud voice saying in heaven saying, "Now salvation, and strength, and the kingdom of our God, and the power of His Christ have come, for the accuser of our brethren, who accused them before our God day and night, has been cast down." So Satan is the Father of Lies and the Accuser of the Brethren. Brethren, meaning sons and daughters of God. So when you forgive someone, you are promising three things: 1)You will not bring the offense up again to the person who offended you; 2) You will not bring the offense up again to anyone else. 3) You will not bring the offense up again to yourself.

How do you recognize unforgiveness when you've been hurt by someone? Take this quiz and find out:

- Do you have strong emotional feelings when you see the Person who hurt you?
- Do you want relationship, or do you try to avoid the person?
- Do you still rehearse vengeance you would like to deliver?
- Do you imagine ways of getting even, getting revenge?
- Can you sincerely bless this person?
- Do you honestly rejoice when good things happen for the person who wounded you?

Some more signs of unforgiveness can be:

- difficulty in relationship with God
- prayers not answered as before
- physical problems
- periods of despondency which quickly return after joyful times
- difficulty sleeping or just resting
- physical, emotional, and mental torment
- continuing patterns of sin or difficulty

Forgiveness is a choice to obey, it is not a feeling. It is not always necessary to feel the anger we've pushed down. It is not always necessary to feel like forgiving. If you choose to forgive, eventually your feelings will catch up with your decisions. So many people come into my office for counseling and say, "When the one that hurt me apologizes, then I will get my life back." And I say, in return, "what if they never apologize"? Then that means that they have already hurt you and betrayed you and have ruined a moment in your life, but now, you are going to give them control of your destiny also?" I have heard it said that holding unforgiveness is like drinking a vial of poison and hoping that your offender dies. The only one that it kills is you. Many times, your offender is off living their life, going on vacation, enjoying life, and you are the only one that your choice not to forgive is affecting. So now, unforgiveness is the toxic waste running through your blood system and is cancelling out your destiny. Is that person that hurt you really worth missing out on all of your blessings? When you choose to forgive, you bring the thermostat back into your own room so that you can decide the temperature of your own life. Choosing unforgiveness and bitterness because we want to feel "in control" actually puts the control into the hands of the other person, because when you have a bitter root towards someone, your emotions are in control and are ruling you. Your emotions are exalted above your decision. When you make the choice to forgive, your emotions are cast in to the sea and cannot rule any longer. Choosing unforgiveness also allows the enemy to control you. The enemy is not omnipresent, or present everywhere like God. He needs connectors to do his evil work on the earth. As long as you don't forgive your offender, the enemy is using you to stay connected to evil against the person you will not forgive.

Basically, the enemy is using your hurt and bitterness to do his bidding on the earth. According to Matthew 18, when we hold unforgiveness towards ourselves, God or others, we are held in a debtors' prison. We put ourselves in there by not forgiving, and we have the key in our hand to go free and let ourselves out of the prison, but we are choosing to stay locked in there because we won't give up our right to be right.

Hebrews 12:14-15 says, "Pursue peace with all men, and the sanctification Without which no one will see the Lord. See to it no one comes short of the grace of God; that no root of bitterness springing up causes trouble, and by it, many be defiled." This verse tells us clearly that when we don't allow peace to rule our hearts and minds, that we won't have revelation and strategy from God because peace is the soil of revelation. It also reinforces the thought that when we have a bitter root, we are like poison to those around us, we begin to infect everyone-even those who had nothing to do with our issue. Why? Because we are allowing the atmosphere of hell to affect us instead of allowing the atmosphere of heaven to change us and bring that into every place we go. The Ichabod Curse is at its worst when we are in unforgiveness and have a bitter root. It says in That, "if a man regards iniquity in his heart, that God will not even hear his prayer." Bitter roots are not the hurtful or terrible things that happen to us, they are our sinful reactions to the hurtful things that others have done to us. Bitter roots operate according to the unchangeable Law of Sowing and Reaping, which cause us to reap in kind, what we have sown. Galatians 6:7 talks about this law. What you do will come back on you. As children, we judge or condemn a parent for a real or perceived wound. E soon forget the judgment, but because it has been planted as a see, which lies dormant until the right conditions arise, as the judgment is reaped, we are going to repeat the every action for which we judged our parent, or we will continue to be wounded in the same way by others throughout our lives. These bitter roots have to be dealt with before I can help anyone do trauma resolution on the trauma and trauma memories. Repentance and restoration from a bitter root is necessary before you can cast out any demons out of a person. Why? Because the demon has the persons agreement through that bitter root.

In the Garden of Gethsemane, Jesus entered into prayer, and because He was fully God and fully man, He transcended time and space and became us... every person past, present, and future. He took into his body all the sins we have ever committed or would ever commit. 2 Corinthians 5:21 says, He, (Jesus) became sin that knew no sin so that we could become the righteousness of God in Him." In the Garden of Gethsemane is where Jesus' will was surrendered to that of the Father, so that we might have a way back to the glory of the Father's heart. Jesus, even though he never sinned, decided that we were valuable enough to be honored by him giving up his life for us. That is how significant you are to God. He took the punishment that had your name on it. The following prayer is one that will help you neutralize your temptation to hold a grudge, become bitter, and not forgive someone. It is one of the most powerful prayers I have in my arsenal and it is only 7 lines. The prayer is as follows:

THE GETHSEMANE PRAYER

"Lord, in compassion, identify me with the heart of the offender with his hurts and his wounds. Bring to death in me that which would declare my wounder As sinful and me as righteous. I am not better than him. I am one with him at the foot of the cross. I cry out, 'Forgive us!' Set us free from the traps of hate. End all one-up man ship between us. Enable me to identify not only with the evil in him but with what you created him to be. Restore us, Oh, Lord."

When you are really angry at someone and want to come together with that person and work things out, but emotions are high, take this prayer and go be alone for a while. Just praying it will bring you in a place where you realize that you need to give up your right to be right in order to restore the relationship again. This will also help you remember that all you have control over is your own response to what the other person has done to you. You have no control over what they may do or say, but you have control over yourself. This prayer will also give you the right attitude of heart so you can be real about what's really going on.

The entire Kingdom of God is a Kingdom of opposites. In order to keep our peace, we have to be like Jesus and master the art of coming in the opposite spirit. He said to "bless those who curse you", "pray for those who despitefully use you". This makes no sense to our natural man. But the spirit, evil or good, finds entrance when we come into agreement with its manifestations. For example, if someone is coming at you with strongholds of intimidation and fear, respond in love. If someone is coming at you with despair, depression and hopelessness, respond in joy. If someone is coming at you in a place of anxiety and panic, respond in peace. Stay in a place of peace when someone in a place of panic and you will shift things with them.

Some examples of this are Paul and Silas in Acts 16, where they were constricted by accusation, pain, and prison. They were beaten with rods and their feet were in stocks, for doing the right thing by preaching the Gospel. Yet in the midst of their accusation and imprisonment, they began to release praise to God. They released the glory of God through the sound of worship. You cannot release the glory of God without the death in the atmosphere being swallowed up. The glory swallows up the oppression. Out of this, the story goes that the prison place shook like an earthquake, and they were set free, but stayed to lead the prison guard to the Lord and then his whole household was saved. What Satan meant for evil, God turned for good because they came in the opposite spirit.

Another example is Joseph, who overcame through faithfulness. Each time Joseph was imprisoned or constricted and those that were supposed to be faithful to him weren't, he remained faithful. God rewarded his faithfulness and this brought forth faithful service and saved his family and many from famine. Then there was David who overcame by trusting God's timing and call, even when Saul was trying to kill him.

The more you get into the habit of coming in the opposite spirit, the more you will want to do it, because you will begin to see the payoff for yourself. You will feel more at peace and more in control of your own response. This will give God a chance to work in the situation also.

If you are struggling with forgiving someone who has hurt you, know that forgiving them doesn't mean you have to let them back in your life the same way they were before. You can create a healthy boundary —not a wall. What I mean by this is that you can decide the levels of access you will give them to you, as trust is rebuilt again. If you go to them and they are willing to work through the issue, then you have won them over and now, you both can go forward and invest in the relationship. Little by little, you can begin to spend time together and rebuild trust. Or you might decide, that because of their unwillingness to work through it with you, that until both sides are cooperating to work to rebuild, that you will maintain a healthy boundary.

Psalm 23:4 says, "Even though I walk through the valley of the shadow of death, I will fear no evil; for you, Lord are with me; your rod and your staff, they comfort me." This verse tells us that in our darkest moment of confusion, infirmity, uncertainty, hardships and broken relationships, that we have Jesus-The Good Shepherd-with us. The shepherd uses the rod, which is the Word of God, toward off his enemies, like Jesus did in the wilderness. The shepherd also used the staff—which is our reliance on the Holy Spirit; that as we choose to lean on the Holy Spirit, He will comfort us.

If this chapter is bearing witness with you and you can see yourself in these pages, and you know you want to make things right on your side, with God, even if the other party never changes, then, do the following steps.

1) Read "The Gethsemane Prayer" mentioned a few pages back aloud.
2) Read the "The Prayer for Bitter Roots" Prayer aloud, filling in the blanks to the prayer, as they pertain to your personal situation.
3) Read aloud the Prophetic Word "This Is Your Passing Through Moment"
4) Read "Decree a Thing" out loud for the next 21 days.

A PRAYER FOR BITTER ROOTS

Lord, I recognize that I have judged

_____ **for**

_____

and I have locked myself into that same behavior and attitude. I choose to forgive him/her for hurting me. I choose to release my right to hold this offense against him/her, knowing it is up to You alone to judge all of us. Please forgive me for the sinful ways I have reacted and for the way sin which I have done the very same to others.(Be specific in naming those you have hurt and how).

Lord Jesus, forgive me for judging

_____.

Now I see I am reaping he same pattern throughout my life. I choose to forgive, and release my anger and bitterness to You, Lord.

Please remove it from my heart. Forgive me also for my part inn tempting

---

to do the very thing I hated by the power of my bitter-root expectations and judgments.

Lord, I ask you to break each judgment that has been named and remove it from me now. I ask You to consume the reaping of all the years of sowing destruction. Replace it with Your blessing. And I ask you to bring experiences in to my life as evidence these judgments are no longer operating. Strengthen me in my inner man to be able to practice new responses. Continue to bring awareness of any other judgments in the perfection of Your timing, Lord.

In Jesus Name, Amen

PROPHETIC WORD
"THIS IS YOUR PASSING THROUGH MOMENT"

And this is what the Lord said: "Say to my people, "Are you going through hell? Then keep on going. Have I not told you in my word, that 'when you pass through the waters, that you will not drown, and when you pass through the fire, the flames will not consume you?' "I tell you there is a PASSING TRHOUGH IN YOUR TRIAL, says the Lord. See yourself as just passing through hell—passing through the water—passing through the fire—I took the keys of hell, and I took the keys of death and the grave. And the enemy cannot lock you up there any longer, says the lord your God. For I created the waters and the enemy cannot drown you there. I am the fourth person in the fire—the flames cannot consume you there. There is a PASSING THROUGH MOMENT in your history, says the Lord. But I say to you, keep on going, keep on moving. Are you going through hell, keep on going, keep on walking. There is a spirit of a finisher in you—because my son, Jesus is in you. He carried His Cross—and He finished His assignment—and You will too. TAKE UP YOUR CROSS AND CARRY IT RIGHT THROUGH HELL—AS DEMONS TREMBLE AT THE SIGHT OF YOU AND MY GLORY THAT YOU CARRY INSIDE OF YOU. For as you do, the gates of hell are swallowed up in my victory. You are passing through, into the dominion, into the authority, into the power and the possession of your rightful inheritance, says the Lord. Take your rightful place for my Kingdom. My Kingdom comes through you—my Kingdom passes through you. As you pass through hell, keep on going, keep on walking, and keep on moving. My Kingdom will become and I my will will be done in your life. As demons shutter at the shadow of my glory on you— all those around you will come into my Kingdom. This will happen because of your choice to keep on going, only as you're passing through this trial, through this moment, through this suffering, and through this season, says the lord. For I say unto you, You are in a wilderness, saying where is the River of Refreshing— and I tell you My Holy Spirit is inside of you. Yield to my Holy Spirit. As you do, You will be the river—in other people's wilderness—you will point them to the question of 'Where is the answer—where is the power and where is the real power and the glory?" It will only be in the name of my son Jesus. You bring the answer. You bring the truth of my son, Jesus, you bring the Word. You bring the help, in the authority of my Name. But as you're moving through this season of hell, keep on moving...For behold—I am with you. I will not leave you or forsake you in your weakness. I am with you and I am for you. You've got this because I've got you."

DECREE A THING

- I triumph over my enemies and over all obstacles because God gives me Victory over every circumstance.
- In all things I am more than a conqueror in Christ Jesus.
- The Lord God goes with me to fight for me against my enemies and gives Me the victory.
- I am thankful to God, who in Christ always causes me to triumph and Rejoicing in victory.
- I decree that the Lord is full of greatness, power, glory and majesty and that He Causes me to be victorious.
- I am not afraid. God is with me to deliver me. He is with me to rescue me.
- I am strong in the Lord and courageous because God is for me and not against Me.

- My heart is confident and secure in the Lord; though there may be tribulation And trials, I do not fear because He has overcome the world.
- I proclaim the greatness of our God and rejoice in Him because he has won the Ultimate and eternal battle for me.

Decrees based on: I Corinthians 15:57; Romans 8:37, Deuteronomy 20:4, 2 Corinthians 2:14, I chronicles 29:11, Proverbs 24:6, Jeremiah 1:8, Romans 8:31, John 16:33, Psalm 18:46-47

CHAPTER SEVEN

SHAME OFF YOU: HOW TO KEEP YOUR HONOR ON

**"Teacher, which is the greatest commandment in the Law?" Jesus replied, "Love the Lord your God with all your heart and with all your soul and with all your mind. This is the first and greatest commandment. And the second is like it: "Love your neighbor As yourself."
-Matthew 22:39-40**

This case study is about my husband and I, and it is not one of my finest moments. However, out of these very tense moments, this chapter and this very powerful prayer tool was born, so it was worth it. It was in the fall about 2 years ago, and James and I were driving down the parkway for our first "vision weekend". A vision weekend for a married couple is when you plan about 3-4 days away for the purpose of praying, relaxing, but especially to get the mind of God on your year and come to agreement about how the next year will be spent before everybody else in your circle decides it for you. If you don't have a plan to meet your goals as couple, someone else will decide what that looks like.

So as we are driving down the parkway, we start to talk about a radioactive topic that we disagree on. So instead of praying, we both begin to go into our case about why we believe our opinion is the right one. So, we pull over to a rest stop to get more coffee, thinking that we just need a break to regroup and thinking it will be better when we get back in the car. We didn't pray at all. We got back in the car and picked up right where we left off. It escalated and now a half hour from our destination, we weren't talking at all. Somehow, I don't think that was the vision God had for our marriage. So, we prayed when we got to our destination, and then went to sleep, hoping that things would be better in the morning. Well, we woke up, and there was still stuff in the air between us. We each took time to pray on our own, cause we could not start talking about our year if we couldn't even have unity on our weekend. As we prayed and came back together, the Lord began to give us scriptures and as we read, he gave us a strategy and keys to help us resolve conflict together.

Out of that weekend, this prayer tool was born. I use it at least once a week when I feel that I am dealing with issues that I really don't have a grid for, or when I am struggling to have the God response for a situation, or when I just don't know what the solution is to a problem. Before I tell you about this prayer tool strategy, I have to explain to you that Jesus modeled for us how to keep a culture of honor between ourselves and others—and he defined what it is by how he responded to others.

I Peter 2:17 tells us to "Honor all people, Love your brother and sisters in Christ. Fear God. Honor the king." In his lifetime, Jesus honored all. He never sought to overpower others or did he allow himself to be overpowered with dishonor or shame even to the cross. He retained His love, forgiving until the work was done.

Traditionally, we think of honor as a concept rooted in hierarchy. This idea has given governments and religious leaders the authority to oppress others with their rule. In this system, the leaders have a voice, and the people do not. This method often uses military forms of intimidation, domination, and control to ensure compliance. Biblical honor is defined as "Kabad", the weightiness of God, the manifest Presence of God, the glory of God. We are all a product of God's love and glory through the finished work of the cross.

To be clothed in honor, we must first put on love. Don't leave home without it. You need to see that the love and honor of the Father that lives within you belongs to you. It is yours to walk in and wear as you choose. You choose love and honor in any circumstance. Colossians 3:14-15, says, "But above all these things put on love, which is the bond of full maturity. And let the peace of God rule in your hearts, to which also you were called in one body, and be thankful." It is our choice to lay down our love in a difficult interaction or to keep it on. In the same way, it is our choice to retain or relinquish our honor where shame is directed towards us.

It is an ungodly belief that to endure the cross, we must wear shame. Hebrews 12:2 tells us that "Jesus ignored, disdained, and disregarded the shame that his fellow Jews attempted to place on him at Calvary." A dictionary definition of "despise" used in this same passage, means to consider worthless, lacking power.

To the natural eye, lacking revelation, Jesus was a pitiful, broken man whose death meant nothing. In the Spirit realm, it was just the opposite. The shame that others layered on him in the natural, found no place in His spirit. Just as death was swallowed up in victory, shame found itself powerless as Jesus took His seat at the right hand of the Father affirming his identity and finished work.

Shame is defined as "a state of being defective or unacceptable or not measuring up to the standard." As believers in Christ, we are accepted in the beloved just as we are. At the Cross while Satan was screaming, "your death is not enough, this pitiful offering has no power, you are defective!", the heavenlies saw it very differently. Jesus was a lamb without spot or blemish. He was the sacrifice to take away the sin of the world. That was His internal reality. Our internal reality is that we are creatures of love and honor. Jesus' death gave to us an inborn strength to overcome shame and retain honor. Jesus example and authority has imparted to us through supernatural love an honor the ability to overcome rejection of family and religious system, to overcome abusive treatment, and to overcome even death. Jesus' spirit never came into agreement with His outer reality.

When we are in the presence of someone who is attempting to strip us of our identity, we have the right to retain our honor. Jesus demonstrated this for us when he stood before Pilate during His trial. John 9:9-11 says, "Where are you from?" But Jesus gave no answer. "Why don't you talk to me?" Pilate demanded. "Don't you realize that I have the power to release you or crucify you?" Then Jesus said, "You would have no power over me at all unless it were given to you from above. So the one who handed me over to you has the greater sin." Here Jesus just let Pilate know that he did not have authority over His life. In an accusatory confrontation, sometimes no answer is warranted, other times a statement of facts is warranted.

Jesus had an internal reality of love and honor, and so do we. From just like Satan tried to layer him with shame, the enemy also tries to do layer us with shame. Jesus had an internal reality and I believe the Holy Spirit helped him keep that intact, even when Satan was trying to strip him of it. In your spirit, you have an internal reality of honor and esteem and love. You have an acceptable place in God's heart. So honor needs to be seen as "a state of being", and not the hierarchal thing that society presents it as. Do we honor authority? Yes. Do we give honor where it is due? Yes. But we need to see ourselves as "honor". We keep this in check by being clothed in love when we are tempted to own the shame that the world, flesh and the devil are trying to put on us.

So how do we do this? Because we know that the devil will keep on trying to tempt us to give up our love clothing and hold onto shame to stop us from the great plan God has for us. So, how do we stay in the spirit, so we don't fulfill the lusts of our flesh? I am glad you asked.

Have you ever seen those commercials that show a heavy person from their newly thing season? Those before and after cases. In the before shot, they look like they are overweight, worn-out, wearing a tent for clothes, and they look like they are death warmed over and are ready to die any second? Then all of a sudden you see them in the after photo, after they have dropped 5 dress sizes, mainly another whole person. They have on a bikini, all tan, hair perfect, teeth white, with enough energy to conquer the world?" Those commercials show about 5 of those weight loss cases, with some hyper-thumping music in the background, and as they come to the last person's before and after photos, all of a sudden, the announcer says, 'TAKE THE WEIGHT OFF AND KEEP IT OFF!!"

Well, I believe that is what this tool will help you do, however, you have to use it on a consistent basis. The name of the tool is "Running To the Mercy Seat Prayer Tool". In Psalm 99:1, it says, "The Lord reigns, let the peoples tremble. He dwells between the cherubim; let the earth be moved." In Exodus 25, the lord tells Moses to make a mercy seat of pure gold to place on top of the Ark of the Covenant.

So he makes a mercy seat of gold and makes two cherubim angels hammered at the two ends of the mercy seat. The cherubim at the two ends of it face one another and the faces of the angels will be toward the mercy seat. The Lord said that he would speak to Moses there, from the mercy seat. In the New Testament, Christ is our mercy seat. Romans 3:23 tells us this. The word for mercy seat is the same root word for "atonement" which means to cover, cancel, appease, or cleanse. Because of the blood that was sprinkled on the mercy seat, man's sin and guilt was washed away and the cure for the law has no effect. So when we are in the middle of our mess, the middle of our confusion, the middle of our problem, the middle of ourcrisis, we can go to our mercy seat, which is Christ, and Hebrews 4: 15-16 says, "For we do not have a high priest who is unable to sympathize with our weaknesses, but we have one who has been tempted in every way, just as we are, yet without sin. Let us then approach the throne of grace with confidence so that we can receive mercy and grace to help us in our time of need." So the following are the steps of the prayer tool and what they mean and how to use them.

Step I - We must come with the attitude I KNOW NOT.

a. ROMANS 8: 24: 'For in this hope we were saved. But hope that is seen is no hope at all. Who hopes for what he already has? But if we hope for what we do not yet have, we wait for it patiently." In the same way, the Spirit helps us in our weakness. We do not know what we ought to pray for, but the Spirit himself intercedes for us with groans that words cannot express. And he who searches our hearts knows the mind of the Spirit, because the Spirit intercedes for the saints in accordance with God's will."

   1. We have to repent and lay down our own wisdom and knowledge and understanding of what we think we know and How we

think we know everything to even pray for. We have to come to the mercy seat and first say, "I KNOW NOT" EVEN HOW TO PRAY, AND WE NEED TO COME AND PRAY IN THE SPIRIT—OUR PRAYER LANGUAGE SO THAT THE HOLY SPIRIT WILL PRAY FOR US AND THEN RELEASE TO US WHAT IS THE FATHER'S WILL. WE CAN'T COME AS IF WE KNOW IT ALL—JUDGING ALL—AND JUDGING THE SITUATION FROM OUR OWN LIMITED UNDERSTANDING. If you do not have a prayer language, ask the Holy Spirit to baptize you with his spirit.

2. WE HAVE TO REPENT OF thinking we know what we are doing. Jesus, on the cross, said, Father, forgive them, for THEY KNOW NOT what they are doing."

When we do this, we let Father know that we cannot—and will not rely on our own ability to deal with our trauma trigger the moment it happens. We have to be convinced that left to our own devices, we will try to use substitutes for the true teacher—Jesus—to teach us what to do. Our substitutes are to self-medicate with alcohol, food, gambling, shopping, chocolate, drugs, television, sex, or just self-justification to retaliate to the other person.

3. WE HAVE TO KNOW THAT JESUS, OUR GREAT HIGH PRIEST LIVES TO MAKE INTERCESSION FOR US. AND WE HAVE TO UNDERSTAND THAT THE TESTIMONY OF JESUS AT THE MERCY SEAT IS THE SPIRIT OF PROPHECY. (Rev. 10:19). So the Father wills, Jesus speaks what the Father wills, and then the Holy Spirit makes it known to us through prophecy. The prophetic word of Jesus releases divine strategy to us, by our exchanging our poor excuse for our own righteousness with the true righteousness of Christ. And as we make this exchange, we take on Christ, our righteousness as we would a robe.

   Romans 12:1&2: says, "Present yourselves a living sacrifice, holy and acceptable before God—which is your reasonable service. Be not be conformed to this world, but be transformed by the renewing of your mind—so that then you may test what is good, acceptable and the perfect will of God."

4. As we run to the mercy seat, and lay ourselves down, as the trigger is happening, and begin to pray in the spirit, we repent of our own knowledge and ways to deal with it or ways to which we push down the pain of it. We literally hand God our lack and we receive His provision of the 7 fold anointing in Isaiah 11. In this

moment, in this exchange, we get the glory of God to fall on us. The glory of God is the full weight of his spirit, counsel, might, wisdom, knowledge, understanding, and the fear of the Lord.

Once we do this, meaning make the exchange, each time you feel a new trigger coming, pray this prayer and make the exchange as quickly as you can. This is the way you resolve trauma or inner conflict, when you are allowing a situation or a person to strip you of your honor. This is how you get your love back on to wear again. You might say, well, what do I mean by triggers? Well, sometimes you will be having an argument with your spouse, or someone else, like James and I were having at the beginning of this chapter on our vision weekend, and we were both triggering out of fear of losing control in a particular area, so our responses were not rational. We were both perceiving rejection from each other. They were attached to some other fear that we each had in our lives. We needed to both get back in the spirit, where the Holy Spirit could lead us into the truth, not our souls fighting to be in control.

So when that subject was brought up, we both were triggering fear. Our minds and emotions started to suddenly look to fight or flight. When this is happening, our soul is in the driver's seat and trying to take over. Triggers happen at the speed of light. So at this moment, it is important to get the mind of Christ and get your spirit man back in the driver's seat as quickly as possible.

In addition to getting a perspective that you are honor—it is your state of being, and you can always use the mercy seat prayer tool when you are really struggling with emotions, or temptations of addictions, etc., I also want to leave you with one more way that you can combat the shame of the enemy.

Another weapon to help you stay clothed in love is to love yourself. I know that this is a very selfish society we are living in—the "selfie era", etc. However, in Matthew 22:39-40, Jesus said "that we should love him with all we are, and then love our neighbor as we love ourselves." How can we love our neighbor, or spouse, or children, of family of God, if we don't love ourselves? Well, we need to keep going back to God's word to reinforce who he really is so we know the honor and the majesty we carry in Jesus.

The biggest stronghold that we all have that keeps us from loving God and loving ourselves is taking the name of the Lord in vain. In Exodus 20:7, it reads, "Thou shalt not take the name of the Lord thy god in vain." You may say, "I don't swear or use Jesus' name that way. Well, if God said, while talking to Moses, in Exodus 3:14, "'I am that I am." Or in another translation, it says, "I am who I am", then say this to the people of Israel I am has sent me to you. "In this passage, God named himself, "I am", which means whatever he needs to be right now. So, every time you say, "I am sick", you take his name in vain. Every time you say, "I am broke", you take his name in vain. Every time you say, "I am losing", "I am a loser", "I am not enough", "I am not smart enough", "I am not gifted enough", "I am not talented enough", you take his name in vain."

What should we be saying instead? You should be saying, "I am blessed,", "I am healed", "I am whole", "I am redeemed". We should be saying, "Everything I need right now, I have right now." Say, "I am blessed and the goodness of God is running me down and taking me over." Psalm 68:19 says, "Bless God who daily loads us with benefits." You're confidence cannot be your social security or unemployment benefits. So even if you mess up today, you wake up the morning with a brand new mercy. You can't talk like the world and choose life at the same time. Every day, the Bible says, "I lay before you, life and death, blessing and cursing, this day, choose life."

Before I give you the tools and decrees for this final chapter, I want to leave you with a testimony from my own life. This was the first time that I realized that what Psalm 107:20 says, which is, "He sent out his word and healed them; he rescued them from the grave", came alive to me. I realized that God was in the middle of my exact situation and cared for me, as an individual.

I married very young and had two sons that were 15 months apart. It was a very difficult marriage and because of my unresolved trauma, and the weight of being a young mother, who was shame based, I didn't want the people in the church to know about my struggle with an abusive spouse, so I buried myself in the ministry in work, in order not to deal with the pain. Shame-based people's cardinal rule in life is to hide the true self so that everything appears to be in order. The Curse of Ichabod, that orphaned heart, due to fatherlessness, was alive and well in me. Now I was married to a man who had actually been left as an orphan by his mother at age one. So the Curse of Ichabod was working in both of us. One Sunday afternoon, after a very bad night with a big fight; I was home with my two sons, they were about 3 and 4 years old. They were taking their naps and I was in my bedroom and I was grieved beyond; I was hopeless, powerless, and was tired of fighting tired. I went in the bathroom cabinet and got a bottle of tranquilizers that I was given for my stomach because my nerves were so bad. I sat on the edge of my bed with the pill bottle in my hand, and with tears in my eyes, I yelled at God and I said, "I am going to take these pills and end it all. I am so sick of all these people that get up at church and tell these testimonies of people who got their own special word from God and how he speaks to them. I said, "where is my word, God? I want my own word from you!! If you really love me, give me a word, and I won't take this bottle of pills, God." Then, from the corner of my eye, I could see my Bible sitting on the night stand. And so, out of sheer desperation, I went over and picked it up and opened it to the first thing I found. (Thank God it wasn't the scripture: "And Judas went and hung himself", or "Go now and do likewise.") I opened up to this section in the Bible, with tears running down my face, pill bottle still in my hand, and as I opened it up, it said the following words:

"Do not be afraid: you will not suffer shame. Do not fear disgrace, you will not be humiliated. You will forget the shame of your youth and remember no more the reproach of your widowhood. For your Maker is your husband—the Lord, Almighty is His Name. The Holy One of Israel is your Redeemer. He is called the God of all the earth. The Lord will call you back as if you were a wife deserted and distressed in spirit, a wife who married young, only to be rejected, says your God. For a brief moment I abandoned you, but with deep compassion I will bring you back. In a surge of anger I hid my face from you for a moment, but with everlasting kindness I will have compassion on you, says the Lord your Redeemer."

In that moment, I felt the heart of a loving father, who heard my cry, cared about my exact situation, and I felt hope pouring back into my heart. I repented for meditating of taking my life, and I laid down on the bed, and decided that it was okay to rest because God met me where I was at, and I could rest safely in his arms. See, this morning, God cared about the corporate body of believers at church as a whole at church. But this afternoon, God cared about me, Kelly, as an individual. That is the heart of the Father we have in God. He cares about everything that concerns us. I think that was the moment that I began to love and respect myself and I started to realize that my voice mattered because God listened to me, heard me, and responded to my heart. When the Ichabod Curse is being broken, it is always because the power of what God has to say trumps everything else. I want you to see that the enemy will always be on the prowl to put shame layers on us, but we have to combat it with the Word of God. Satan will always cast doubt and say, "Did God really say", and our answer always has to be, "It is written". I leave you with those three very powerful words to live by.

The following steps are so that you can begin to quickly move yourself out of triggering negative emotions that keep you from staying clothed in love and honor.

Step I: Read "Running to the Mercy Seat Prayer Tool" aloud. And deal with a current issue on your heart right now.

Step 2:   Read "When I Love Myself" declarations aloud for the Next 21 days. As an activation, ask the Holy Spirit to Reveal to you which one of these declarations you Are struggling with in the area of loving yourself. Ask Holy Spirit to begin to help you in that area. Healthy love gives and takes, not just either, or. Ask Holy Spirit to heal your love receptors so that You can begin to enter into a deeper connection With God and others.

Step 3: Read the prophetic word aloud.

Step 4: Pray the A.M. and P.M. prayer daily to keep yourself walking in the spirit connected spirit to spirit with God, in the spirit of peace, which is the soil of revelation.

RUNNING TO THE MERCY SEAT PRAYER TOOL
By Prophet Kelly McCann

Dear Heavenly Father, in this moment, with my desperate situation of (name the issue), I lay myself and all my emotions down before you—I give you my emotions of (name the emotions you are feeling), in clear view of your mercy, Oh, God, which is Jesus Christ.

I come to your mercy seat, and I repent for my own pride in my own wisdom, knowledge and limited understanding. Left to my own knowledge, I will make the wrong choice and do the sinful thing right now. I repent for walking in the letter of the law that is killing me and everyone around me. I repent for all hyper grace that says because your grace abounds, I can keep on sinning, and have no responsibility for my actions, even though your Word says that I need to work out my own salvation with fear and trembling before you, and with you, Oh, God.

So, Father, as I lay myself down, I say, 'I KNOW NOT" how to pray. As Jesus stated on the cross, "I KNOW NOT WHAT I AM DOING" right now...with this current issue, condition, situation and/or relationship. But I know that I am the temple of the Holy Ghost. Therefore, I decree that I know not how to pray; and as I open my mouth, I choose to let the Holy Spirit pray for me. (Pray in the spirit now for about 1-2 minutes).

I thank you that I can exchange my filthy rags and put on your righteousness, which is Christ Jesus. Now that

I am in right standing, out of that position, I can know what is the good, and acceptable and perfect will of you, Father, for this situation. Thank you, Jesus that you sit at the right hand of the Father to intercede for me. As you pray the will of the Father for me right now, the Holy Spirit makes it known to me and is giving me the power and courage to carry it out.

Thank you for your blood sprinkled on the mercy seat and thank you Jesus, for your blood poured out at Calvary—and for being my great high priest, who forever lives to make intercession for me. (Lift your hands) As I lift my hands up now, I ask you, Jesus, to cover me with your blood, and I ask you Holy Spirit, to release the power in the blood of Jesus to help me exchange my lie for the Truth. Truth is a person called Jesus Christ. I willingly take Him on me and proudly walk in the confidence of who I am in Him.

Holy Spirit, as you are revealing to me the will of the Father for this situation, now give me the courage to do it. Thank you—I receive it now.

Father, be glorified in my choice.

AMEN.

(Whenever you use this tool to break the power of triggers, always replace it with a blessing..read psalm 91 and decree it over your life aloud.)

WHEN I LOVE MYSELF DECREES

1. When I love myself, I realize that God broke the mold when he made me. There is NO ONE ELSE like me in the whole world.

2. When I love myself, I know that I was created with the right face, height, hair and body shape. God made me BEAUTIFUL.

3. When I love myself, I am willing to expose my hurts, weaknesses, and faults. My inner self, my spirit man, is the real me. I live in HONESTY.

4. When I love myself, I understand boundaries, mine and yours. I walk in HONOR with myself and with others.

5. When I love myself, I no longer second guess my decisions. When I walk with God, I am at the right place, at the right time with the right heart. I walk by FAITH.

6. When I love myself, I do not have to please others. I do not fear rejections ,obligations, or expectations. I walk in CONFIDENCE.

7. When I love myself, I will steward my time in things that bring me joy. I can move in my divine pace that is neither too slow or too fast. I DANCE to the RHYTHMS of Heaven.

8. When I love myself, I can freely shout, sing, dance, and laugh. I was created for FUN.

9. When I love myself, I can be alone and not be lonely. My BEST FRIENDS are me and God.

10. When I love myself, I take care of my health, body, and mind. I break addictions and temptations that poison my life. My body is the TEMPLE of God. God's best for me is always higher than what I think is best for me.

11. When I love myself, I do not have a poverty spirit. I am free to like beautiful things, go on vacations, and eat good meals. I am RICH in God's eyes.

12. When I love myself, I no longer remain in my past or worry about my future, but I live in the present. I am FREE.

13. When I love myself, I recognize my unique gifts and talents. I have a DIVINE PURPOSE.

14. When I love myself, I don't have to listen to my worst critic, me. beating myself up is no longer allowed. I live in GRACE.

15. When I love myself, God's Word outweighs the attacks of others. No one stands over me, I stand TALL in God.

16. When I love myself, I forgive others. Unforgiveness only hurts me. I FORGIVE.

17. When I love myself, I no longer have to prove myself. I am already IMPORTANT AND HONORED AND LOVED.

18. When I love myself, I can love others, I can love God.

19. When I love myself, I don't sell myself short. I CAN DO THE IMPOSSIBLE WITH GOD.

THE PROPHETIC WORD

'HAVEN'T I TOLD YOU IN MY WORD AND STATED, AND DECLARED, TO YOU THAT 'AS I AM IN THIS WORLD, SO ARE YOU.' I TELL YOU, 'I AM NOT SCARED', 'I AM NOT SICK', 'I AM NOT CONFUSED', 'I AM NOT OVERWHELMED' WITH THE CARES OF THIS WORLD; 'I AM NOT IN LACK', 'I AM NOT DEPRESSED', NO, I TELL YOU THAT I AM THAT I AM. WHEN YOU CAN SAY WHAT YOU ARE THEN YOU CAN SEE WHAT YOU ARE. YOU ARE WHO I SAY YOU ARE. YOU ARE WONDERFULLY AND FEARFULLY MADE. YOU ARE MY BELOVED CHILD. YOU ARE SEEN. YOU ARE REDEEMED, AS ONE PULLED FROM A BURNING BUILDING. YOU ARE RESCUED FOR A HIGHER PURPOSE. YOU ARE SPECIAL AND SET APART FOR MY GLORY. YOU ARE MY GLORY AND MY JOY, BECAUSE YOU CARRY MY NAME. YOU CARRY MY GLORY ALWAYS, BUT YOU RELEASE MY GLORY WHEN YOU SAY WHAT YOU ARE TO ME. WHEN YOU SAY WHAT YOU ARE TO ME, THEN YOU WILL SEE IT AND MY GLORY WILL BE SEEN BY THOSE AROUND YOU."

THE A.M. AND P.M. PRAYER

The A.M. Prayer – Every day you wake up, pray this prayer. Doing this every day will begin to put your spirit man back on top and close to Daddy God. Doing this will also put your body and soul (mind, will, emotions) beneath your spirit. Your spirit is the part of you that communes with God, discerns good and evil, and Possesses divine authority in God to bring heaven to earth in every circumstance. This prayer will start your day off right by having your spirit in the driver's seat And your soul in the passenger seat.

"Lord, I consciously call my spirit to attention. I want to hear your voice. I want to commune with you right now. I bless my spirit to lay down every thing I do not need to process right now. I bless my spirit to connect with you, Father or Lights, who sees all things. You know what I'm dealing with in the spiritual realm. Father, I just come into complete peace with you and your Spirit in me, right now, to hear you. God, just open the communication lines between your spirit and my spirit right now. Thank you Daddy. Amen"

The P.M. Prayer – Your spirit interacts with God in the night seasons. Psalm 16:7 says, "Even at night my spirit instructs me." At night our soul is muted because it relies on our bodies to be fully engaged. Your spirit can interface with the spirit of God while sleeping. When you are sleeping, your soul is not cognizant or aware of your surroundings. Your soul sleeps when your body sleeps with regards to your environment, yet your spirit remains awake. Job 33:14-16 tells us, "For God may speak in one way, or in another. Yet man does not perceive it. In a dream, in a vision of the night, when deep sleep falls upon men, while slumbering in their beds, then He opens the ears of men, and seals their instruction." Based on these truths, pray this prayer every night before you go to sleep to get answers to problems, new revelation, creative ideas, and downloads from heaven for your life and for those you serve with your life.

"Father, I thank you for this day. I ask my soul to step aside and I instruct my spirit man to come forward and to set aside all that it is processing at present. I instruct my spirit to connect with you, Father God, spirit to spirit. I ask you to reveal to me all that you want to work on now to bring me into a deeper revelation of your love, and purpose for my life. Father, I thank you that, as I sleep, you open my ears and seal my instructions from you. I will rest in the joy of who you are, my Lord and King, and in your sacrifice, I am set free. Amen."

THE END

If you have enjoyed this book, please tell your friends to read it and also, if you have comments or for bookings for events, please visit my website at www.truecolors8.com or email me at: kmcdrawn2him@yahoo.com or you can also like us on True Colors Ministry, International on Facebook.

NOTES

Patricia King, "31 Decrees of Blessing", 2016, p. 88, p. 40 (used for Decrees on chapter 1 and chapter 5 of Birthmarked)

Paul Cox, "Come Up Higher", 2010, p. 66-67, (used for explanation For Jante Laws in chapter 5 of Birthmarked)

John Sanford, "School of Prayer Ministry", 2009, p. 59, (used for 'The Gethsemane Prayer' in chapter 6 of Birthmarked)

Hino, David, "When I Love Myself" eblog, 2015, (used for "When I Love Myself" decrees in chapter 7 of Birthmarked)

Aiko Hormann, "Healing Tools", 2005, (used for "The Reason We Clap" in chapter 5 of Birthmarked)

CPSIA information can be obtained
at www.ICGtesting.com
Printed in the USA
BVOW06s1420160118
505364BV00001B/4/P